HOW TO PLAY PIANO FOR BEGINNERS KIDS

A Definitive And Complete Piano Book
For Learning To Play

DAVID NELSON

CONTENTS

PREFACE

Music is an interesting subject because it has for long and still is part of our existence, somehow we can agree that it's rather difficult to define our lives or tell our stories without a bit of the experience of music here and there. Man has evolved and so has music, it's safe to say that man and music are one and the same. The slow but consistent growth of music has forced us to seam the art into the fabric of our culture, making music more than just a subject but for a certain fraction of the world and in some climes, it is a culture! And culture being a summary of our unique ways of living, music is now a way of life.

The purpose of this book is not far from the concocted love and admiration for the art called Music. The love and practice of music has in times past and until now helped a great deal of artists communicate their passion through rhythms, lyrics and sublime compositions and musical pieces that we still appreciate today. From classical composers like Mozart, Beethoven to contemporary

1

composers like Yanni and a host of many others around the world, the influence of music is still very much heated, generation after generation. This book aims to introduce to you the art of Music, its history and how it's made particularly with the Piano.

This book therefore offers more than just an introduction, it is in fact, a guide for piano lovers and enthusiasts to find usable texts and information on their journey to becoming a master at playing and composing awesome musical pieces. The information herewith, is targeted at beginners and those with no formal education on music and how to play the piano. As a guide, this book will begin from the subject of music, how it has evolved over the years, the different types of instruments used to make music before seeping into the fun waters of the piano as an instrument, what it's made of, how it was invented and particularly HOW TO PLAY IT!

The journey to being an expert starts with a decision to learn the basics, before you can fly you must first learn how to crawl. Invariably, to become an expert at playing the piano, you must first learn the basics, not just learning but adding consistent practice as an ingredient to the puddy. This book offers that opportunity, first to learn the rudiments of music and the piano instrument, then the slow and steady guide on how music is made using the piano. As a music enthusiast, I have watched myself navigate the murky waters of learning and practicing and today saddled with the privilege to share what I know. I do hope that this book offers great help on your journey to becoming a great piano player!

CHAPTER ONE :

The piano as a musical instrument

What is Music?

Music is a group of sounds that people have arranged together in a pleasing or meaningful way. Music in fact, means different things to different people of the world cutting across race, religion, culture, language and country. What is interesting however is that all countries and cultures of the world make some form of music, when Nigerians make music, it is called Nigerian music, when Americans make music, it is called American music and the famous Indian music made by the Indians.

Another interesting fact about music is that it is a language itself, yes! Music is a universal language spoken in sounds, rhythms and beats. Music can be simple — for example, one person whistling through the mouth, another person tapping out a beat on a container or log drum, or as simple as listening to the chirpings of the birds. Music can also be complex — for example, hundreds of instruments playing together for hours in a large opera hall. Music is fun!

Today, as in the ancient times, people use music for different purposes as well as in different occasions. We have music in schools, we have music in the military, we have music in weddings and other ceremonies and we have music in films! There are sad music, joyul music, thoughtful music, dramatic music and so on. All the different kinds of music just have a way of eliciting certain human emotions and help us understand what the performer or composer is trying to communicate.

Before we explore the piano as a musical instrument, let us take a look at what music was like in the past, a brief history of music and what music is to us now, shall we?

History Of Music

Have you ever wondered how Music was like in the ancient times? The kind of instruments they used? Who taught the ancients how to sing? Who made the first instruments? And other bothering questions. Let us learn the History of music, citing important dates from history in the making of what music is today.

Percussion instruments made up most parts of the earliest music forms, simple instruments like rocks, sticks and metals. These simple instruments are believed to have been used in most ceremonies or for war cries. At that time, there were no music texts or writings of any form, only sounds made from the crude music instruments. The South Americans, the Aztecs, Native Africans and Red Indians were foremost practitioners in the use of music for religious ceremonies and rituals.

The advancement from crude musical instruments to more advanced ones did not begin until 4000BC, and it started with the Egyptians;

4000 BCE - The Egyptians invented harps and flutes and by 3500 BC, they developed an instrument called lyre and the also first clarinet.

The Egyptian lyre and flute

2500 BCE – In Denmark, the first trumpet was developed, we call it the "natural trumpet" now. It is entirely different from modern day trumpets. It is valveless, and requires the use of the lips to change pitch.

The natural trumpet

1500 BCE - The Hittites crated one of the most important musical instruments today, the guitar! Yes the Guitar. In music, this was a major achievement because the guitar uses frets to change pitch by plucking a string or strings. This advancement led to the development of other vibrating string instruments like the violin and the harpsichord.

800 BCE - The first ever sheet of recorded music was found, a religious musical hymn. However, it was written in cuneiform (cuneiform is an ancient style of writing that uses symbols instead of words)

700 BCE - Records of songs that included vocals with instrumentals were found. This was the birth of accompaniment type of music where people sang songs and instruments played.

600 BCE - Pythagoras, a Greek philosopher developed the octave scale. In Greece at that time, music was a passion because they had a lot of free time helping them cultivate artistic skills.

400 BCE – Greece hosted trumpet competitions as part of their many events.

350 BCE – Aristotle, another Greek philosopher developed music notations and layed the foundation for theoretical music. His work is still studied till today.

In AD 521 – Boethius introduced the Greek system of music notation to Western Europe. This helped them develop native folksongs representing their lands. Boethius also was the first to write about the idea of an opera.

MUSIC IN THE MIDDLE AGES

After the fall of Rome, most of the music created then was curated by the church, the Orthodox church. The Orthodox church particularly the Catholic religion has a long history with the musical arts. In AD 600, Pope Gregory built the Schola Cantarum in Rome it was the first music school in Europe. The choir comprised of about twenty to thirty men and only those who were skilled in singing were selected to perform with the Schola Cantarum.

In China, music was also advancing, in AD 612 there were reports of orchestras with over a hundred musicians performing for the several Chinese dynasties at time.

In AD 650 , a new sytem of writing music was developed known as 'neumes'. The neumes served as a sort of notation for groups of notes in music. The first neumes were derived from Greek texts. The neumes were further modified into shapes indicating pitch direction. Neumatic notation was later used in medieval music to show patterns of rythms, this later developed into the musical notation we have today.

After the Schola Cantarum was built, 144 years later, another music school was opened in the Monastery of Fuda, it was a singing school. By AD 790, there were annexes of the Schola Cantarum in France. In AD 800, Charlemagne the great unifier developed poems and psalms that were set to music.

In AD 850, musicians from the Catholic church invented the "modes" The modes later developed into the major and minor scales we have today.

In AD 855, the first polyphonic piece was recorded, the polyphonic is a piece of music written for more than one voice part.

In AD 1000, Guido D'Arezzo, an Italian music theorist improved the music theory. He reworked neume notation by adding time signatures, hence, he's best remembered as the inventor of the modern musical notation. After that, he invented the solfege. The solfege is the vocal note scale: do, re, mi, fa, so, la ,ti, do.

The Musical instruments

When humans moved from making sounds with their bodies, for instance, by clapping with the hands, to using objects around them to form music from sounds, musical instruments were born, a musical instrument was thus, known to make sounds pleasing to the ear. The earliest musical instruments were designed to sound like natural sounds, and the purpose of music at that time was for religious practices like rituals other than entertainment.

Musical instruments are today constructed in different styles, sizes and shapes, using different materials. Early musical instruments were derived from "natural objects" like shells and wood, and as the making of musical instruments advanced, so did the kind of material used advanced. It should however be known that almost every material in nature today has been used by at least one culture of the world to make musical instruments. Music and nature are one!

People use their mouths to sing however, to make other kinds of music they need different musical instruments. As a definition, musical instruments are tools people use to make music. A person who uses musical instruments to make music is knows as an *instrumentalist*. Musical instruments can be grouped in four broad categories: wind instruments stringed instruments, percussion instruments and electronic instruments.

Knowing the different classes of musical instruments will help you determine which instrument among the different classes is best suited for the kind of music you want to make.

Let us discuss the instruments one by one:

String instruments: These instruments work with a very simple principle; they produce sound wave vibrations by strings. With the understanding of music, notes and rhythm, a good string instrumentalist can make good music with the right combination of several strings at the same time. Examples of string instruments are guitar, violin, harp etc.

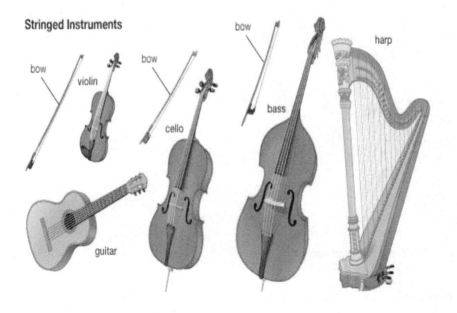

The stringed instruments

Wind instruments: This class of musical instruments require the use of the mouth to blow air into the instruments to produce the desired sound. The sound is created by a stream that flows through or around the body of the instrument. Examples of wind instruments are, trumpet, saxophone, flute, clarinet, trombone etc.

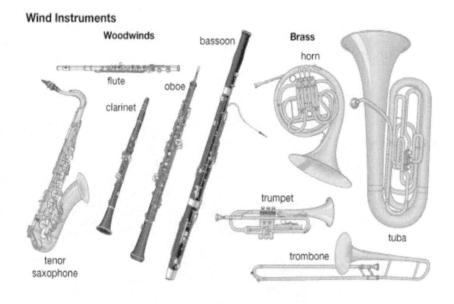

Fig 1.1 The wind instruments

Percussion instruments: Percussion instruments are those that require you hit or strike their surfaces to produce the desired sound.

They generally make a sound when they are struck, shaken, scraped, plucked or rubbed. Instruments that fall under this category include the xylophone, the piano, the tambourine, the drums etc.

The percussion instruments

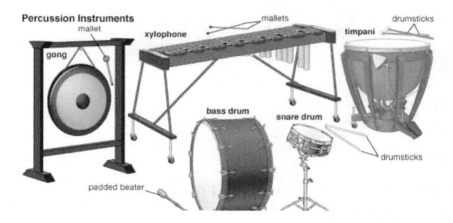

Keyboard instruments: This class of instruments uses the latest technology to help people produce sounds. The instruments operate in a way that makes it easy for anyone to produce sounds. These instruments are played by pressing down the keys. The keys control a mechanism that produce sound. Electronic instruments include keyboards, organ, harpsichord, etc.

Keyboard Instruments

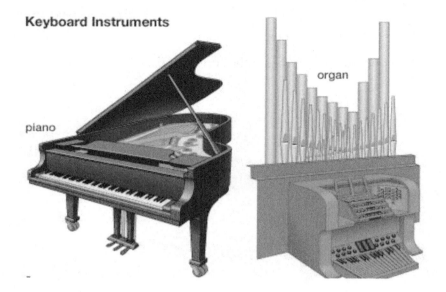

The keyboard instruments

HORNBOSTEL–SACHS CLASSIFICATION OF MUSICAL INSTRUMENTS

In 1914, Eric Von Hornbostel and Curt Sachs published a new scheme for classifying instruments. This classification scheme was an adoption of Mahillon's classification scheme.

According to Hornbostel–Sachs system of classification, musical instruments are didvided across four main groups:

Idiophones – According to them, idiophones are the instruments that produce sounds by vibrating the body of the instrument themselves;

they can be further subdivided into plucked, percussion, concussion, split, shaken, scraped idiophones. Examples are the xylophone, slit drum, rattle etc.

Membranophones – Membranophones produce sounds by vibrating a stretched membrane, in the case of a drum, the membrane is the drumskin. Sounds can be produced by the membranophone by striking the drumskin with a stick or with the hands, or by rubbing the surface of the drumskin with the hand or another object. Examples are the snare drum, timpani, kettle drum, barrel drum etc.

Chordophones – A chordophone is a string musical instrument. Sounds are produced by the vibration of a stretched string or strings. Harps, guitars and violins can all be regarded as chordophones. The vibration of the strings when the instrument is played is resonated by the hollow in the body of the instrument. The strings can either be plucked (harp) strum (guitar) or rubbed with a bow (violin). Even the piano is sometimes regarded as a chordophone because of the assemblage of strings in the piano that are struck by hammers to produce sounds. Examples of chordophones include, cello, double bass, violin, ukulele, viola, guitar, banjo, piano, etc.

Aerophones – These are the wind instruments. They produce sounds primarily by the vibration of a body of air. This is done most times by the transfer of air from the players mouth into the instrument without the use of any object. They can be further subdivided into, free, non-free, reed, reedless, brass aerophones. Examples are, clarinet, trumpet, accordion, harmonica, recorder, saxophone, whistle, trombone etc.

Mentioned above are the major classes of musical instruments. It is advisable to determine the kind of music you wish to produce to ensure you learn the instrument that perfectly fits you. This will allow you become the kind of musician you have always dreamed.

The piano.

The piano is an acoustic, stringed instrument invented in Italy by Bartolomeo Cristofori round the year 1700, a very while ago. It is played using a keyboard, a row of keys that a performer presses down or strikes with the finger of both hands to cause hammers in the piano to strike the strings.

The word piano may be a shortened sort of *pianoforte* and it refers to the variations in volume produced by a pianist's pressure on the keys with his hands: the greater key press, the greater the force the hammer hits the strings, and the louder the sound of the note produced. The piano was created as a contrast to harpsichord, a musical instrument that does not allow variation in volume as the piano; compared to the harpsichord, the first pianos in the 1700s had a warmer and quieter sound.

An acoustic piano usually features a protective wooden case surrounding the soundboard and metal strings, which are strung under great tension on an important metal frame. A padded hammer in the piano strikes the strings once the white or black keys on the keyboard are pressed. The hammer rebounds from the strings, and therefore the strings still vibrate. The vibrations are passed through a bridge onto a soundboard that amplifies by more efficiently converting the acoustic energy to the air.

You can also sustain notes through the use of the pedals positioned by the bottom of the piano. This pedal is referred to as the Sustain Pedal and it allows pianists play musical pieces that would have been impossible. Unlike the organ and harpsichord, two major keyboard instruments widely used before the piano, the piano allows variations of volume and tone consistent with how a performer presses or strikes the keys.

Most modern pianos have 88 black and white keys, 52 white keys for the notes of the C major scale (C, D, E, F, G, A and B) and 36 black keys, which are raised over the white keys. That way, over 88 varying notes can be played on the piano, from the highest treble to the deepest bass.

As you know, there are white and black keys on the piano and each serves different functions. For the black keys, this includes what are known as 'accidentals': G♯/A♭, F♯/G♭, D♯/E♭, C♯/D♭, A♯/B♭ and (we will learn about the accidentals in subsequent chapters), which are needed to play in all twelve keys. Although an acoustic piano has strings, it's usually classified as a percussive instrument instead of as a musical instrument , because the strings are struck instead of plucked.

According to the instrument classification system of Hornbostel-Sachs, pianos belong to the class of instruments called chordophones (chordophones are a class of instruments like the percussion, they produce sounds by striking their surface). There are two main sorts of piano: the grand and the upright piano.

There are varying using for grand piano. It is useful across various genres of music including but in no way limited to: chamber music, art song, and classical solos, and it is often used in the jazz and pop style of music.

The more popular type of piano, however, is the upright piano. Its compactness and portability makes it ideal for domestic practice in private dwellings.

HISTORY OF THE PIANO

Innovations like the forged iron frame in the 1800s enjoyed major influence from the Romantic music era and its musical trends. This development gave grand pianos a more powerful sound, with an extended richer and sustained tone. A family's piano in the 19th century played an equivalent role that a radio played within the twentieth century; when a nineteenth-century family wanted to listen to a newly released musical piece, they could hear it by having a family member play it on the piano (how interesting). During the nineteenth century, music producers produced many musical works in arrangements for piano, in order that music lovers could play and listen to the favored pieces of the day in their different homes. The piano enjoys wide usage in jazz, traditional music, pop and jazz for solo performances, accompaniment, and for composing, songwriting and rehearsals. Although the piano is extremely heavy and expensive (in comparison with other widely used instruments, like the acoustic guitar), its musical versatility (i.e., its wide pitch range, ability to play chords, louder or softer notes and two or more independent musical lines at an equivalent time), the massive number of musicians trained in playing it, and its availability in performance venues, schools and rehearsal spaces have made it one among the Western world's most familiar musical instruments. (The Americans call the Piano the King Of All Instruments)

The piano was invented using technological innovations in keyboard instruments. Pipe organs have been used since the ancient times, and as such, the development of pipe organs enabled instrument builders to learn about creating more sophisticated keyboard mechanisms for sounding pitches. During the Middle Ages (a very long time ago), inventors tried to replicate and create stringed musical instruments with crude tools like struck strings.

The mechanisms for the inner workings of the keyboard underwent a major development in the 17th century when the harpsichord and the clavichord were developed. In a harpsichord, the strings are plucked by quills mechanically when the performer presses the keys while in a clavichord, the strings are struck by tangents.

Centuries of labor on the mechanism of the harpsichord especially had shown instrument builders the foremost effective ways to construct the case, soundboard, bridge, and mechanical action for a keyboard intended to sound strings, hence the invention of the PIANO.

INVENTION OF THE PIANO

The invention of the piano is today credited to Bartolomeo Cristofori (1655–1731) of Padua, Italy, who was employed by Ferdinando de' Medici, the Grand Prince of Tuscany, to be the Keeper of the Instruments. Cristofori was an expert in the making of harpsichords, and was well vast with the knowledge on the shape, size and body of stringed keyboard instruments; this knowledge of the keyboard outlook and how it works helped him to develop the first pianos. Cristofori named the instrument, the first piano he made 'un cimbalo di cipresso di piano e forte' meaning ("a keyboard of cypress with soft and loud"), abbreviated over time as pianoforte, fortepiano, and simply piano as it was adopted later.

Cristofori's became famous and successful when he designed a stringed keyboard instrument. This produced richer notes when the hammer is struck. It was a bit of a dicey situation because the hammer must hit the note a certain way and it must not stay together for long or else this would stop the sound and stop the strings from vibrating and making any sound.

Therefore once the hammer strikes the string, it must be raised or lifted above the strings so that the sound can have perfect resonance. Moreover, the hammer must return to its original position without bouncing off violently, and it must return to a position in which it is ready to play almost immediately after a key is depressed so the player can repeat the same note as quickly as possible . In the next century, Cristofori's piano action design became a model for many approaches in the making of the piano actions.

The instruments made in Cristofori's early years were mainly constructed with thin strings. These instruments were softer and way quieter than the pianos available today, but they were much louder and with more sustain in comparison to the clavichord, the clavichord is perhaps the only previous keyboard instrument with the same ability to as the piano in terms of weight of sound. While the clavichord allows control of volume and sustain, it is however quiet. The harpsichord on the other hand produces a sufficiently loud sound. The piano can perform the best from both instruments, combining the ability to play loudly and perform sharp accents.

The piano is an example of a musical instrument and popularly known as the Mother of all instruments because no matter what type of music you love, your favourite songs sound better on the piano. From our discussion on the different classes of instruments, we know that the piano is a percussion instrument, that is, it requires that you strike the surface to produce the desired sound. The piano is a very fun instrument and comes in several sizes to help those who would love to learn how to play.

The piano is made up of several parts; most important are the keys that make the piano a piano. The keys are coloured white and black and are arranged on a straight line on a wooden base. A standard piano has 88 keys, 56 white keys and 32 black keys. We will learn more about the keys as we progress. It should be noted that one who plays the piano is called a Pianist.

Types of piano

There are three primary types of pianos: the grand piano, the upright piano and the electronic piano. All three types of piano have their similarities and differences, and found in different places like homes, churches and schools. Learning the different types of piano will help you identify them wherever you find them.

Grand piano: Grand piano are the largest piano types, they are also the most majestic and expensive. The outer part of the grand piano is made of wood while the inner part comprises of strings, reinforced wood and small metal reinforcements. The keys of the grand piano are made from ivory; the grand piano has the standard 88 keys. However, the grand piano can take up a lot of space because of its large size. In grand pianos, the frame and strings are horizontal, and the strings extends away from the keyboard. The action can be found under the strings, and returns to rest by using gravity. There are various sizes of the grand piano:

Baby grand (about 1.5 meters high)

Parlor grand, or boudoir grand (about 1.7 to 2.2 meters high)

Concert grand (between 2.2 and 3 meters)

Longer pianos with longer strings have larger and richer sounds. Pianos with short string scales and thicker string have more inharmonicity, which is the degree of sharp sounds produced by the piano. The greater the inharmonicity, the harsher it sounds to the ear.

One of the principal reasons why full-size grands are used in the concert hall is their ability to produce brilliant sounds and sustained tone quality. Smaller grand pianos satisfy the needs of domestic use; as well, they are used in small teaching studios and smaller performance venues.

The grand piano

Upright piano: The upright pianos are the most common type of pianos. This is because it is cheaper than the grand piano, it is smaller in size and produces warmer sounds. Like the grand piano, the outer part of the upright piano is made from wood with a little metal reinforcements. The upright piano also has 88 keys and the keys are made from ivory.

Upright pianos are also called vertical pianos and are more compact due to the vertical structure of the frame and strings. The structure and the action of upright pianos was first invented in London, England in 1826 by Robert Wornum, and from then, models of the upright pianos became the most popular piano model. Upright pianos took up less space than a grand piano, and as such they were a better choice for use in private homes for domestic music-making and practice by kids and piano enthusiasts. The hammers move horizontally, and return to their rest position via springs. Upright pianos with long strings and unusually tall frames are usually upright grand pianos. Some writers classify modern pianos according to their height and according to the modifications of the action that are necessary to accommodate the height. Upright pianos are less expensive than grand pianos. Upright pianos are used in churches, community centers, schools, small music halls and are also used as rehearsal and practice instruments, and they are popular models for use in homes.

Upright pianos like the grand pianos come in different types; Console pianos and Studio pianos.

Console pianos, which have a more compact action and shorter hammers. Console pianos are a few inches shorter than the studio pianos. Studio pianos on the other hand are around 107 to 114 cm tall.

The upright piano

Electric piano: The electronic or digital piano has the feel of the other types only that the outer parts are most times made from plastic. The electric piano is suitable for beginners and they are usually most affordable. The electric piano is different form the grand

and upright pianos because it uses power supply and is technological compared to the other two types. The electric piano has the advantage of allowing the user to practice silently with headphones so as not to disturb people. With advances in technology, the amplified electric pianos were created in 1929, the electronic pianos created in the 1970s, and the digital pianos created in the 1980s have all been developed. The electric piano became a popular instrument in the 1960s and 1970s because of the of jazz, funk and rock styles of music. The first electric pianos made during the late 1920s used metallic strings with a magnetic pickup, an amplifier and a very loudspeaker.

Electronic pianos are considered non-acoustic since they operate without hammers or strings like the grand and upright pianos, the electric pianos uses synthesizers that simulates piano sounds using filters that synthesize or blend the sound of an acoustic piano.

Electronic pianos have to be connected to a keyboard speaker or amplifier to produce sound although most electronic keyboards come with inbuilt speaker and amplifier.

Digital pianos are also non-acoustic like the electric piano and do not have strings or hammers. They use digital technology to reproduce the acoustic sound of each piano note accurately. Like the electric piano, they must be connected to a power amplifier and speaker to produce sound however, most digital pianos have built-in amplifier and speaker. Digital pianos also make use of pedals, like the sustain pedals.

The electric piano

Parts of a piano

The human body has several parts both external and internal. The external parts are the eyes, ears, nose, mouth, the hands and legs while the internal parts are the kidneys, the lungs, the heart, the stomach. The same applies to the piano, the piano has several parts, both internal and external parts and each of the parts has its function. Let us examine the parts of the different types of piano, starting with the Grand piano

The Grand piano

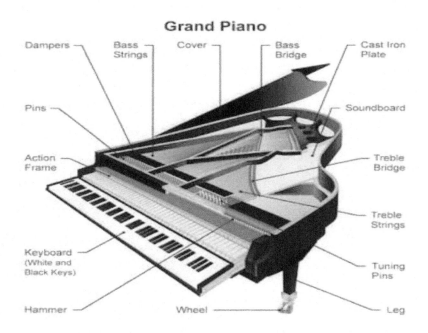

Fig 1.6 The parts of a grand piano

Action frame: A thin stretch of wood that is tightly fixed to the piano to help with the playing of the piano .

Dampers: They are triangular felts that help with the vibration of the strings

Bass strings: The bass strings are like a winding wire made of steel used to slow down the vibration.

Cover: The cover is like a lid used to cover the keys when the piano is not in use.

Bass bridge: Like a bridge, the bass bridge links the sound from the vibrating string to the bass body.

Cast iron plate: The cast iron plate sustains the tension of the strings even when the tension tends to be massive.

Soundboard: The soundboard is also known as the belly, it is the large wooden diaphragm inside the piano.

Treble bridge: They are long narrow wooden rails stretching from the soundboard and guides the strings when they vibrate.

Treble strings: Treble strings are wires beginning at one tuning pin, round a hitch pin and back to where it started.

Tuning pins: The tuning pins are steel pegs that are usually one and a half inches long everywhere a string is wound.

Leg: The legs are a wooden patch that forms the foundation for the piano, they add beauty to the instrument.

Wheel: The wheels are used for moving the piano around.

Hammer: The hammer is like a mallet covered with felt and used to produce sound by striking the strings when a key or keys are pressed.

Keyboard (white and black keys): The horizontal stretch of keys that make the piano what it is.

The upright piano

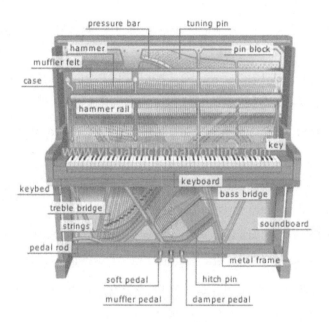

The parts of the upright piano

Hammer rail: The hammer rail is where the hammers in the piano rest.

Case: The case is the well decorated wooden house of the keyboard

Muffler felt: The muffler felt is the lowered cloth between the hammer ans the strings that gives a muffled effect on the sound.

Pressure bar: The pressure bar prevents the strings from moving sideways..

Tuning pins: The tuning pins are steel pegs that are usually one and a half inches long everywhere a string is wound.

Pin block: The pin block is a large piece of hardwood used to anchor the tuning pins, it is also known as the wrest-plank.

Strings: The part of the piano that is struck by the hammer to produce sound.

Keybed: This is where the action, keys and keyframe rests inside the piano.

Keyboard: The horizontal stretch of black and white keys that makes the piano what it is.

Pedal rod: The pedal rod are levers under the piano and controlled by the fet when playing to make the sound softer.

Treble bridge: They are long narrow wooden rails stretching from the soundboard and guides the strings when they vibrate.

Treble strings: Treble strings are wires beginning at one tuning pin, round a hitch pin and back to where it started.

Soft pedal: The soft pedal is one of the three pedals and is mostly used for post-classical sounds.

Muffler pedal: The muffler pedal is the middle pedal that is rarely used.

Damper pedal: The damper pedal is the most used of the three pedals and is used for almost every kind of music.

Hitch pins: The hitch pins are a strip of diagonal metal pins that attach the strings to the ends.

Bass bridge: Like a bridge, the bass bridge links the sound from the vibrating string to the bass body

Soundboard: The soundboard is also known as the belly, it is the large wooden diaphragm inside the piano.

Metal frame: The metal frame is also called the plate, it is mostly used to support both ends of the strings and help them withstand tension.

How the piano works!

The different notes and sounds produced by the piano are the results of strings that vibrate. The strings are forced to vibrate when they are hit by a hammer or hammers all within the piano. The piano has a total of 88 keys and all the different keys play a different note. Although, multiple keys can be played at the same time, like three notes to form chords and create harmony.

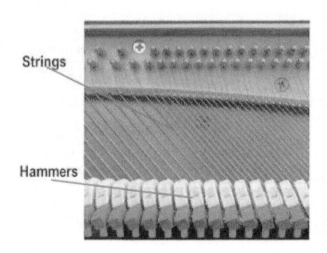

The strings and hammers of a piano

When a key or keys is pressed on the keyboard f the piano, a small hammer located inside the piano hits a string or a group of strings. Every key of the keyboard is connected to its own hammer or hammers and each hammer hits a specific string or a specific number of strings. When a hammer hits a string, it causes the string to vibrate and forced to make a sound that is tuned to a particular note. The strings' vibration is further transferred to the soundboard located inside the piano underneath the strings, when this happens, the soundboard resonates. It's the piano that gives each piano its own exclusive sound and it also helps for sound amplification, that is, make the sound louder.

THE HAMMER

The piano hammers come in different sizes. On the piano, the hammers on the bass side are the largest — they are so because of the kind of deep sound they force the strings to produce, to move the heavier bass strings of the piano, they must have a large mass. Moving towards the treble part of the piano, that's the part of the piano that makes softer sound compared to the bass side, the mass of the piano hammers decrease in size. The hammers on the farthest treble end of the piano are smaller in size and more pointed than the larger and bigger bass hammers.

However, over a period of continuous playing, the hammer felts can become more compacted from the repeated striking of the wire strings. When the damper pedal is pressed down, the hammers and the action of the piano are moved to the right, thereby, allowing the hammers to strike the strings with a different part of the hammer head felt, this operation produces a different tone. A piano technician uses a dedicated tool to soften the hammer head felt, when the technician does this, it is called voicing.

THE KEYBOARD

The keyboard is perhaps what makes the piano what it is. The keyboard is that horizontal panel on which white and black keys finely arranged. Most pianos nowadays feature 36 sets of black keys and 52 of the white. Older pianos however had only 85 keys. The white keys are laid out in rows while the black keys are seen in groups of 2s and 3s (In subsequent chapters, we will find out why the keys of the keyboard are arraigned the way they are)

Long ago, when piano construction started, the keys of the keyboard were made from sugar pine (sugar pine is a type of wood). From 2010 till date, they are usually made of spruce (spruce is another kind of wood). However, because of its pristine nature, spruce is used for high-quality pianos. The black keys were originally made of ebony, and the white keys were covered with ivory. However, since the trees that produce ivory are now endangered, the makers of the pianos now use plastics. Piano making companies like Yamaha invented a kind of plastic called Ivorite that they claim looks and feels like ivory.

Since then, other piano makers have imitated Yamaha in the use of Ivorite.

The Damper

In addition to the hammer, there is also a damper. The damper is covered with felt and its function is to keep the strings from vibrating when they are not being played. When you press a key on the keyboard, the damper is raised from the string to allow it vibrate. When you release a key, the damper moves back on the string and stops it from vibrating.

The damper felt of the piano

The Pedals

There are two or three pedals in every piano generally, and these pedals are controlled using the feet. The pedal to the right is the most commonly used and it is called the damper pedal. It lifts the dampers from all the strings when you press on it allowing the notes to be continued or sustained even after the key is released.

The pedals of a piano

The other two pedals on the left both have different functions depending on the piano. The pedal on the leftmost side is called the soft pedal. It gently moves the hammers for the music to sound a bit softer. It moves the hammers sometimes closer to the strings or a bit to the side. The middle pedal is the muffler pedal and it generally lifts the dampers for the notes being played at the time. It occasionally just lifts the dampers for the low notes to sound depending on the type of piano.

Fun facts about the piano

- The piano instrument is generally used by composers when composing or writing music.

- Because of its vastness, the piano is sometimes called the Mother of all instruments or the King of all Instruments.

- A piano needs tuning twice every year.

- In the last 60 years, pianos have not been made from ivories, rather they are being made from plastic.

- The greatest pianos ever made are known to be the ones made by Steinway. (Steinway is an American company that makes pianos)

- The piano is a very complex instrument. The grand piano may be made from over 7000 total parts.

- Different strings in the piano all have variant thicknesses to get different notes. Low notes have thicker strings.

- The working part of the piano is called the action.

- The first pianos were too expensive for even the very rich people to own.

- A new piano should be tuned at least four times a year to adjust to its new environment and ever changing seasons. After the first year, tuning it twice every year is fine.

- Modern pianos have a cumulative number of 88 black and white keys.

- When seated at a piano, the deepest bass (bass is a deep sound) range is the first key on your left, and the highest treble (treble is a light sound) is the last key on the right.

- The piano can be considered both a string and percussion instrument (Most recognize it as a percussion instrument because hammers strike the strings inside to produce sound)

CHAPTER TWO:

Piano habits

In this chapter, you will be taught the correct posture to maintain anytime you play the piano, the good and bad habits of learning the piano and the golden rules you must follow to be a professional piano player.

Posture

Place the piano bench according to how wide the keyboard is, that is, the width of the keyboard. The bench must face the piano completely. Sit at the front half of the bench, this will keep you to steady your feet. Relax your feet on the ground and keep them flat on the ground. Ensure your weight is resting on your buttocks. Relax your shoulders and keep your back straight.

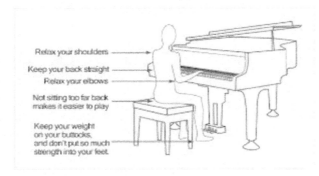

The correct posture when sitting at the piano

Place both hands on the keyboard, imagine holding an object like an egg, and imagine it being cradled on your palm. This is the right hand posture to assume while playing the piano. It helps relax the hands and it also allows you to play smoothly. And most importantly, keep your nails short!

Hand Position

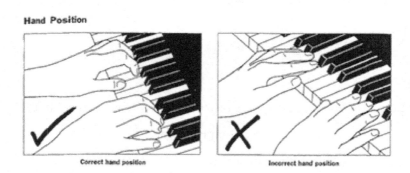

The correct hand position when playing the piano

Please do not play with your fingers flat – if you do, your hand may not be flexible and you might never be able to play anything fast.

Although the fingers should be directly above the key, and ensure you touch only the key that is being played.

Things to remember;

- Always play with clean hands and short fingernails
- Always check that the chair or piano stool is at the centre of the keyboard and at the right height.
- Always make sure you are sitting correctly
- Always listen to every sound you make on the piano.
- The bench or piano stool should not be higher than the piano.
- Do not play with flat fingers. Your fingers should be curved as if holding an egg.
- To make loud and impressive sounds, you need the whole weight of your arms not your fingertips.

Good and Bad piano habits

Habits are those things we do repeatedly that make us better or worse at something. Hence, we have good and bad habits, the good habits help us become better while the bad habits make us worse at what we do. For example, there are good and bad health habits, brushing your teeth and taking a proper bath are considered good health habits while eating without washing your hands or wearing dirty clothes are considered bad health habits.

The same applies with learning the piano. There are good and bad habits, the good piano habits help you become a great piano player, while the bad habits take you one step behind that goal every time you practise them.

Let us start with the bad habits. These piano habits are all easy to pick up, however, learning about them will help you spot them and prevent them from happening.

Bad piano habits

- Playing too fast or too slow: Playing too fast is probably one of the most common mistakes pianists make. It tends to happen when you first begin to learn a new piece, because you are eager to play it at the correct speed. The best way to learn anything is go very slow at first and only begin to increase the speed once you can play it without any mistake. Another common bad habit is to play the most of the piece at the correct speed, but the difficult parts at a slower speed. This only confuses the brain, so it is important to find an average speed that you can play the whole piece at.

- Playing too loud or too quiet: Unless you have a great ear to hear your own mistakes, this is an easy habit to pick up. Many pianists play too loud or too quiet and the reason is that there is no one to tell them. To help with this bad habit, you can record yourself as often as you play or get a friend to help you, so that you can always listen back and fix the problem if you play too loud or too quiet.

• Sitting too far from or too close to the piano: Although, this habit is easy to rectify but it still happens among pianists. Ideally, you would want to sit far enough from the piano keys so that your arms are parallel to the floor. If you are too close then your elbows will be sticking up slightly and will be too far back which will mean you are hunching over the keys. It's best not to sit too far from or too close to the piano.

• Incorrect posture and hand positioning: This tends to happen when you don't practice scales and certain exercises which are essential in moulding your hand around the keys. Beginners usually play with the top of the hand leaning either down or to one side. To check whether you have a good hand posture, place a coin on the back of your hand and play a scale. If you keep the coin from falling off, then you should have a good hand posture.

• Incorrect practice routine: This final habit is one of the most important to consider, and ties in with the 'playing too fast' habit. When you practice it's important to take things really slow at first, and gradually build up the speed without making any mistakes. It sounds simple, but it's something which is missed by a lot of pianists. There are vital routines present when practising, and a lot of people miss them out with through laziness or frustration. To get better at anything, you need to always push yourself during practice routines and be disciplined about them. You can also include easy sections too, to keep your motivation level high.

Next are the good piano habits, these habits when practiced repeatedly help you become a great pianist. By learning the habits and doing them, you can take you piano playing to a whole different level, like a professional!

Good piano habits

- `Great pianists prepare the environment for practice, because distraction breaks your concentration. By preparing the environment, great pianists come well rested, they wear comfortable clothes and their pencils and notepads ready. They avoid distractions like TV, video games and playtime with friends.

- Great pianists take care of their assets, in this case it's the piano. One can spot a great pianist by looking at the way they treat their assets. Great pianist clean and polish their pianos and ensure it's in the best condition for practice.

- Great pianists warm up before playing, yes! Just like athletes, great pianists understand how important it is to warm up the muscles before playing or practicing.

- Great pianists analyse their mistakes after every practice. They do this by taking breaks to check if they made any mistake, like playing too fast or too slow. Great pianists know that making mistakes and learning from the mistakes only make them better pianists. So they are never afraid of criticisms!

- Great pianists set goals and crush them! Let's be honest shall we? When you sit in front of the piano, do you have a specific purpose in mind? Or do you practice aimlessly? When you practice without a clear purpose in mind, it will bring you nowhere and is worse than not practicing at all. Great pianists practice with clear objectives in mind and make sure they fulfil it.

- Great pianists never stop learning! Yes! Very important is the desire to know more. Great pianists always seek instructions and guides on how to become better. They take advice from their teachers or tutors.

- Great pianists love what they do and this helps them practice with enthusiasm and cultivate new ways to boost their motivations. Like watching films about music or discussing with friends what they learn during piano lessons.

The Golden Rule

Practice is a word that is dreadful to most students around the world, it is most times considered scary because of the degree of discipline required. Practice is simply a deliberate effort aimed at learning a particular skill by repeating over and over again, in this instance the skill involves learning how to play the piano. The word practice itself gives a hint into how unpleasant the learning process can be, because it requires a certain level of physical effort to learn how to play the piano, not just physical but also mental too. A required level of concentration is also needed to master the art of the piano. But then, the good news is, once you can take your mind off the gruesome task of learning and focus on the joy of one day being a master, the journey would be a lot easier. It's just like learning how to play football, or learning how to ride a bicycle, it may seem daunting at first but after a period of consistent practicing, you gradually become better and one day very good at it.

Practice is not the same thing as playing. Practice is conscious while playing is unconscious. Playing is regarded as the unconscious reproduction of something you've learned and in this case, playing a piano piece you have learned overtime. It's like preparing for an exam, there will be a time when you just read and prepare, you learn the formulae, you read your notes just to understand, and when examination comes, you find it easy to write down everything you have read overtime almost unconsciously because it has become part of you. It's the same thing with practicing and playing the piano, to be a very good player is sort of the reward of consistent practice.

To know how to practice effectively is halfway through the journey of becoming a very good piano player, while the other half is actually playing the piano. For practicing the piano, there is a golden rule of practice that is designed to guide you through the process of learning, and in the end, following the rule will help you master written music. Here's the golden rule;

STOP! BEFORE YOU MAKE A MISTAKE

It's a rather simple rule, as you learn a piece (be it a pattern, scale or chords), do not allow your fingers play a mistake, a mistake could be, playing a right note or wrong note with the wrong finger. When you do this, you will find out that you always know if you're playing slowly enough or when you're about to make a mistake so you can nearly always stop yourself in time before playing a mistake.

Why then is this rule so important? it's a fact in psychology that the human brain (which in fact is what you train and not your fingers) does not know the actual difference between right and wrong notes. The brain only learns what you do. And in cases where you do something continuously in repetition, whether right or wrong, the brain will learn it even better. Also, if you stop playing before making a mistake, the brain will automatically not learn the mistake!. Just in case you make mistakes (everyone makes some, even the very good players) know that, it will take the brain a much longer time to unlearn a mistake than to actually learn how to play the right notes and use the appropriate fingering. Learning and obeying the golden rule will help you save time during practice sessions and also help you learn master pieces, chords and even other musical instruments faster.

The Importance of Concentration

One very important key to learning and mastering the Golden Rule successfully is concentration. A few dedicated minutes of focused practice can accomplish what an hour or days of thoughtless and aimless practice would take. However, concentration is just like anything else, because the longer you practice concentration the longer and better you will be at actually concentrating. This trick will help you in practicing anything including the piano and also help you in other areas of your life. Just in case you find yourself losing concentration here and there, it's okay to take a few minutes of recess before you continue practicing. No one can actually concentrate without taking breaks.

3 Steps for mastering the Golden Rule

Outlined below are three easy steps for applying the Golden Rule effectively:

1. Play slow to play correct. It's advisable to start at a speed or tempo at which you can comfortably play with each hand separately without making any mistakes. Play as fast as you can play correctly, no

rushing. The moment you can comfortably play correctly at a given speed, then you can try to go a bit faster the next time you practice and if you find yourself making mistakes again, slow down again!

2. You are permitted to pause, if you're not sure of the next note. Take your time to find the right note and begin to play the part of the music before you paused.

3. Very important, do not practice when you are tired or when you find it difficult to concentrate. You need to be mentally alert when you practice and of course need a wholesome amount of concentration to guide you in the process.

To become a great piano player like some of the greatest piano players in history, players like Mozart or Beethoven, here are some rules you must strictly adhere to. Here are a few things to consider;

- **PRACTICE TIMES**

Aim to practice at the same time everyday, for instance, a few moments after you finish your homework or after dinner. This will help you get into a routine and develop a good practice habit.

- **EVERYDAY**

Like they say, It is actually better to practice everyday for 10 minutes than to practice for one hour in a week. You can keep a diary close to you anytime you practice, in the diary you mark the attendance by yourself, and try to practice everyday.

- ## EXERCISE

Practice some easy exercises or scales to get your mind and body back into the idea of playing and practicing. Exercises like locking your 10 fingers and whirling them for about a minute or two, this will help make your finger muscles flexible and ready to go!

- ## WORK!

Spend sometime practising the hard stuff! Be strict with yourself and try to get it as perfect as possible. But do not be too hard on yourself when you don't get it. If you find a piece or exercise difficult, keep practising it over and over again until you notice the improvement, it's the only way you will get better at it.

- ## BREATHE DOWN

Play something you know very well and enjoy playing (this could be simple songs). This will help you relax your mind, especially if you have trouble rehearsing something difficult.

- ## EVALUATE YOURSELF

After playing a piece, ask yourself if what you played was good , what was bad as well as what could be improved. Try to concentrate on the things you could improve on rather than just playing aimlessly.

MAINTENANCE OF THE PIANO

Like a farmer to his tools for working, so is the pianist to a piano. Using the example of the farmer, the farmer knows that to get maximum benefits from the tools he uses, he need to take proper care of them, he knows he needs to sharpen his cutlasses and fuel is tractor. The piano is the tool a pianist uses to create good music and hence, deserves to be taken care of and properly maintained.

The piano is a heavy, powerful and delicate instrument. Overtime, professional piano movers have developed special methods for transporting the grand and upright piano due to their heavy sizes. The methods prevent damage to the piano's outer case and other internal mechanical elements that make up the piano. Part of the maintenance routines for the piano is tuning, this is done to help the piano maintain a consistent pitch. For the piano to function properly and to maintain optimal functionality, it has to be maintained, that is, the inner mechanisms that make the piano work, like the hammers, dampers and strings must be checked and regulated from time to time. Worn out pianos can be repaired and reconditioned by professional piano repairers. The worn out piano strings must be replaced. Oftentimes, by replacing the worn out parts, and reconditioning them, old pianos can perform as well as newer ones. However, like other home appliances, the piano should be dusted, cleaned and prepped for the next practice! In most cases, the pianos are covered with a strip of cloth to prevent dust and mechanical damage to the body of the piano.

Piano Tuning

The process of piano tuning involves adjusting the tension of the piano strings with a wrench specially made for tuning. The process involves aligning the intervals among the tones of the piano so that the instrument is in tune. Guitar and violin players can by themselves tune their own instruments, however, pianists need to hire a piano tuner, a specially skilled technician, to tune their pianos. The piano tuner uses a set of special tools in tuning, the basic tools for piano tuning include the tuning hammer or tuning lever, different types of mutes and a tuning fork. The tuning hammer or tuning lever is used to turn the tuning pins thereby increasing or decreasing the tension of the string or strings being tuned. The mutes are used specifically to hush or silence the strings that are not being tuned.

A piano tuner at work

When a piano is in tune it means that there is a smooth interaction among all the notes that make up the chromatic scale. This scale is different for every piano hence, the need for the piano tuner to always tune the piano to a designated standard called the 'Temperament system'. The temperament system is a tuning system that tempers the intervals, in most cases the perfect fifth (In the coming chapters, we will learn about the intervals), the perfect fifth is said to be tempered when it is narrowed by flattening the upper pitch or slightly raising the lower pitch

Piano tuners basically use their ears when tuning a piano to make sure it sounds tuned. This most times involves them tuning the high-pitched strings slightly higher and lowering the low-pitched strings.

CHAPTER THREE:

History Of The Musical Scale

The musical alphabet serves as the designation of all musical sounds, and it consists of the fisrt seven letters of the alphabet, A , B , C , D , E , F, and G , H in addition, In Germany. In the natural scale, without flats or sharps, the correct order of the letters is C , D , E , F , G , A , B (or H in German), then C. To understand this arrangement, let us briefly discuss the history of the musical scale.

In 595 BC, Isidore, the Bishop of Seville discovered that the oldest harps at that time had seven strings and the shepherds' pandean pipes had seven reeds. Hypothetically, it was believed that the ancient natural scale consisted of seven sounds.

The seven sounds were used for both voices and instrument and were gradually added to, until 340 B.C. during time of Aristoxenus, there were fifteen sounds. The fifteen sounds extended from the A in the first space of the bass section of the grand stave to the A in the second space of the treble stave. These sounds are given distinct names and they were derived from the length and position of the different strings of the lyre.

The ancient Greek authors expressed them by using certain letters of the alphabet in order to avoid writing them in full. However, the distinct properties of the notes varied with the different modes and mutations, which by that time had already been introduced in the musical system. The letters used by the Greek authors were written in a variety of forms, both large and small, some were inverted, others were turned to the right or left, some were expressed as lying horizontally, and several of them were accented in many ways, etc. According to Alypius, the most intelligent of the Greek authors who wrote them tried to explain the musical scale using those letters written in different forms, and so, the musical signs used during his time were not less than 1204, and from written records, that number was soon exceeded.

The Romans borrowed ideas from the Greek scale, and named each of the fifteen sounds in Latin. However, they did adopt the complicated style of the Greeks by using symbols, instead they used the first fifteen letters of their alphabets, A to P to represent the fifteen different sounds. In AD 590, Gregory the Great who was elected Pope at that time discovered that the second part of the scale H to P was only a repeat of the first part, A to H. He therefore ruled out the last eight letters and used the first seven two times (A to G).

He represented the lower octave using capital letters and the upper octave with small letters.

However, the original idea of the Greek scale was maintained, and hence, the letter A was naturally applied to the first and lowest note. About the beginning of the 10th century, another note was introduced and located one degree below the lowest A, this note was at that time called after the Greek letter Gamma and written as (Γ). Many other notes were added to this time after time until Lazarino reached the lower C in the early parts of the 16th century. And thus, the modern music scale was established, and A which was originally the first became the sixth, that is, (C , D , E , F , G , A , B , C)

In Germany also, the same scale system was originally adopted, but when the accidentals were introduced, and it became a custom to sing in certain instances B flat (B ♭) instead of the natural B (B♮), the square shape of the natural sign was soon transformed to the letter H and this was applied to the natural B, B♮ (the original B), and the rounder form of the flat was given the name of B, this distinction is still I use in Germany till today.

The Music Alphabets

Just as children learn the 26 alphabets in elementary school, the world's famous piano players also learnt the music alphabets at a point in their training. Yes! The musical instruments and not just the piano have alphabets and they are easy to learn. It is therefore important that we learn the alphabets before we learn how to play the piano.

The different notes used in music are most times named with certain signs and symbols, these signs and symbols are also called the MUSICAL ALPHABETS. These musical alphabets are important not only when you play music but also when you discuss music and describe the musical notes with your friends, it makes the knowledge of music easy to learn and share.

THE 12 NOTES: THE BUILDING BLOCKS OF MUSIC

Music basically is all up of notes, notes are like the smallest indivisible components of music, the same way atoms are to chemical elements and syllables are to words. A note is simply any pitch or range of pitch made by a musical instrument, meaning, the sound(s) you hear when any musical instrument is played is called a note.

In music, there are 12 notes. But of course we know that there are more than 12 keys that make up the piano, however, there are only

12 notes to be learned and they are pretty easy. You might ask however, "Why then are the keys on the piano more than the notes on the keyboard? The reason is that the 12 notes only repeat themselves again and again on the piano keyboard in different octaves (we'll learn about the octaves)

The 12 notes are categorized into two types; the Natural notes and the Sharp notes. Let us start by discussing the natural notes;

NATURAL NOTES: Every note in music has a letter attached to it, the letter represents the name of the note. And we use the first seven letters of the English alphabet (A to G) to represent the names the notes. It goes from A, B, C, D, E, F to G. When the notes are named using the alphabets, they are called natural notes. Thus, natural notes are just like regular notes.

This is so because when we play the notes the way they are in order, the note that would have been called "H" sounds like "A", we just start the set all over again. For example:

A B C D E F G A or **C D E F G A B C**

This set of eight notes is called an Octave. When you reach a higher note with the same letter name, it will still be an A note but the pitch will be on a higher octave.

SHARP NOTES

Asides the seven natural notes (i.e. A , B , C , D , E , F, and G) there are five notes that fall in between them. These five notes are named as sharp or flat notes. These sharp notes indicate if a note is above one of the natural note while the flat notes indicate if a note is below one of the natural notes.

When you listen to music, most times you hear sharp and flat notes without knowing. Musical notes that are flattened or sharpened are also known as Accidental notes. The accidental notes helps musicians and music composers add spice to their music, they also help musicians who play different instruments talk about music easily, yes, that's right! Accidentals help musicians speak the language of music. Virtually all musical instruments can play accidentals, in fact, when you see the keys of the piano you have seen the sharp and flat notes, you just do not know what they are. The sharp and flat notes can be easily identified on the keyboard as the black keys while the white keys represent the natural notes that is, A B C D E F G.

The sharp and flat notes can be identified by symbols;

The SHARP NOTE can be identified by the symbol (♯). It resembles a hash symbol. To sharpen a note means to go one note higher in pitch than the natural note. For instance, "A♯" a sharpened note (it is pronounced as "A sharp") is one note higher than the natural "A". when the sharp symbol is In front of the natural A, it will then be referred to as A sharp. The sound of the notes A and A♯ are quite different.

Simply put, a sharp note is a raised pitch, or when a natural pitch is raised to the next consecutive pitch. The symbol used to denote a sharp note only notifies us of a slight change in the normal conditions.

THE FLAT NOTE

The flat note is more like the opposite of the sharp note. The flat note is a lowered pitch or when a natural pitch is lowered to the next consecutive pitch. Simply put, just like a flat tire that goes down, that's the same way flattening a note sounds like.

The FLAT NOTE can be identified by the symbol (♭). It resembles the lower case/small "b". To flatten a note means to go one note lower in pitch than the natural note. For instance, "B ♭ " a flattened note (it is pronounced as "A flat") is one note lower than the natural "B".

The symbol used to represent the flat note simply notifies the musician or instrumentalist that the note has changed a bit, and that it should be played as a flattened/ lowered note.

Sharp notes and "Flat notes can also be used as verbs. When you use the sharp note, the pitch is raised by one note and similarly, when we the flat note is used, the pitch is lowered by one note.

The Grand Staff And The Order Of Sharps And Flats

GRAND STAFF

When setting up a jigsaw puzzle, you set the borders first so that other pieces can fit in appropriately, the borders therefore serves a foundation on which the pieces can be arranged. For piano music, this foundation is called the Grand staff. The grand staff is an array of lines and spaces, it comprises of two staffs with five lines each and are both connected on the left hand side by a brace.

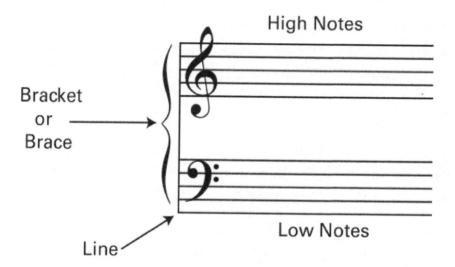

Just as a captain is to the crew in a ship, so are the clefs to the notes on a staff. Without the captain on a ship to give orders, the members of crew will be confused and walk around aimlessly. In the same way, without the clefs, the notes on the staff have no meaning and the staff will only be an array of meaningless lines. On the top staff, the clef there is called the Treble clef, and its purpose is to tell your right hand what and what to play on the piano. At the bottom staff, we have the bass clef, and alternatively, the bass clef tells your left hand what and what to play on the piano.

The function of the clefs on the grand staff is specific, they tell what notes are on the staff and their names too. If you notice the curlique of the treble clef, the manner it goes round the second line from bottom, telling us that the line is G, that is why the treble clef is most times called the G clef. In the case of the bass clef, you see the two dots on both sides of the second line from the top, telling us that the line is F, that is why the bass clef is also known as the F clef.

The notes of the names on the piano run from A to G and then start all over again. The different lines and spaces of each of the staff do the exact same thing, but the note 'A' is not located at the bottom of neither staff. For instance, the lines on the bass staff from bottom to top represent the notes G – B – D – F - A, which can be remembered by using the popular phrase 'Good Boys Do Fine Always.' Similarly, the spaces of the bass stave from bottom to top represent the notes A – C – E - G and can be remembered by using the popular phrase, 'All Cows Eat Grass.'

For the treble staff, starting from the bottom to the top, the lines of the treble staff represent the notes E – G – B – D - F, and can be remembered by using the popular phrase 'Every Good Boy Does Fine.' While the spaces of the treble clef represent the notes F – A –C - E, like FACE from bottom to top.

If you look closely, you will notice a big gap in note names between both the treble and bass staves of. The bass staff ends with A while the treble staff begins with E, so what about B , C , and D? The B note is placed directly above the top line of the bass stave, D is placed in the space that is directly below the bottom line of the treble stave. What about C?

When we exhaust spaces or lines above or below either of the two staves, we use what we call ledger lines to temporarily adjust the staff to make the staff bigger. The C note in between the two staves is called the middle C, and can be written anywhere on either the top or bottom staff.

The Grand staff as we know (or Great stave as it's popularly called in Britain), is a combination of two other staves put, usually the treble clef (G clef) and the bass clef (F clef).

This combination of clefs, that is the combination of the treble and bass clefs is widely used for various instruments, including the piano, pipe organ, the harp, and many more. Both staves can and should be played by one person at the same time, therefore, it's important to know both clefs and also be comfortable reading both of them.

So what then is the importance of using a grand staff? Wouldn't it be better and simpler to just use a single clef, or use the clefs differently?

To answer the question, let's use the piano to explain. We know that the piano has a huge range making one clef insufficient. For instance, if we choose to use only the treble clef, we would need not less than 11 ledger lines whenever we want to plat the C note, yes! That many ledger lines.

Also, going back and forth between clefs will not work, why? Because the piano as we know ois an instrument played with both hands. The left hand needs to play the low notes while the right hand plays the high notes. The solution therefore is to use a Grand staff, which can accommodate two staves comfortably, one on top and the other below. Most of the time, the top staff is the treble clef and the bottom staff is the bass clef. This combination allows us play the low notes as low as we want with the left hand and the high notes as high as we want with the right hand, all at the same time!

The same technique works for other instruments with a wide range like the piano (mostly keyboard instruments and percussion instruments that can be tuned). The grand staff helps to provide access for the player to the full range of the wide ranged instruments just like the piano.

USING THE GRAND STAFF

The Grand staff technique is very common in almost every style of music, from classical music to jazz, to rock, pop, and even in studio music, etc.

Some of the many instruments with wide ranges that use the Grand staff include: Piano, electric keyboards, church organs, harp, accordion, marimba, Hammond organ, etc.

The two different staves on a grand staff are linked by a vertical line on the left side of the bar. All the bar lines in music runs through both staves, joining them into one big and giant staff, hence, the name, 'Grand staff'.

The two staves, the bass and the treble staves are also joined by a brace on the left side. The brace connects the two staves and its function is to remind us that two staves are expected to be played by the same instrument.

In order to read music successfully from a grand staff, it's important for the player to be comfortable reading from both treble and bass clefs individually. The daunting task therefore for any player, is to be able to read successfully from both staves of the Grand staff. As we know also that practice is very key in mastering the piano. The tough things that look difficult at first will turn out to be very easy with consistent practice.

One area where most beginner players find difficult is the Overlap, where the two staves meet. The truth however is, the two different staves do not actually connect with each other. Each of them can still act alone, by itself.

For example the middle C note can be written on either the upper treble staff, or on the lower bass staff and not directly placed in the center, between the two staves. However, there are some other notes that can be written on either staff like the middle C. Specifically, the notes around G3-F4 oftentimes appear on either one of the stave. Although, it takes time in practice to get used to this.

The upper staff, that is the treble staff is meant for notes to be played by the right hand, while the lower staff or the bass staff is for notes to be played with the left hand. In order to avoid confusion, you should first be clear and decide which hand you need to to use to play the notes, after which you then write them on the respective staff associated with that hand, the left hand for the lower staff and the right hand for the upper staff.

For example, the note E4 can be written on any one of the staff. But first we need to decide which hand we will use to play it. If we want it to be played with the right hand, we would write it in the upper treble staff but if we want it to be played with the left hand (maybe because the right hand is busy playing something higher up), then we would write it in the bottom bass staff.

Sometimes a grand staff may contain two bass clefs, or two treble

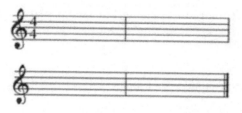

clefs

This usually happens when both hands are playing in the same pitch area of the particular instrument. For example, if the left hand is supposed to play higher than normal, it's also normal to use a treble clef even at the bottom staff instead of a bass clef. Also, if the right hand is supposed to play lower than normal, the top and bottom staves might use bass clefs.

Even in cases as mentioned above, where both hands use the same clef, it is still wise to leave them as different staves so the player is not confused as to which hand to use when playing different notes. Also, when you try to fit in all the music of both hands into one staff, it will be jammed like sardines and would make music very difficult to read, much less play!:

For the pipe organ instrument, whether it is a church organ or the hammon organ used in Rock music, we usually have a grand staff with 3 staves. The top staff for the right hand, the middle staff for the left hand while the bottom staff is used for the pedals, which are controlled by the feet of the piano player. The organ player as to play from all three staves at once!

The bottom staff for the pedals uses a bass clef, and Just like the normal grand staff, the three staves are joined on the left side by a bar line. However, just like the normal stave too, only the top two staves are joined by a brace. The bar lines also, they only connect the top two staves and not the bottom staff.

Here's how it looks like;

The aim of this design is to remind us that the first two staves are for both hands, which work together when playing, unlike the pedals which are controlled by the feet of the player.

DETERMINING THE NAMES OF THE LINES AND SPACES

When we try to determine the different names of the spaces and lines of the Grand Staff, we simply use the correct sequence of the musical alphabet (A B C D E F G) and apply them to the lines and spaces of the grand staff.

For example, we know that the second line from bottom line in the treble clef is known as the "G" line. The next space directly above it would the "A" line (this is because "G" is the final letter in the music alphabet and after it is "A", so the alphabets simply repeat over again).

Having that in mind, the next line directly above the "A" space in the treble clef is called the "B" line. And the space directly above the "B" line is called the "C" space and so on. The notes placed on the lines or in the spaces are given the corresponding names as we follow the sequence of the musical alphabet.

The dia gram below shows the naming of the spaces and lines of the Grand Staff.

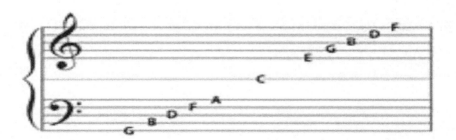

Notice that between the two staves is labeled "C" it's called the Ledger line. It functions as a link bridge between the two staves, and the note usually placed on this line is popularly known as "middle C ".

In my intention to help better understand the notes on the lines and spaces of the grand staff, here's a traditional method to aid in memorizing the names and notes of the Grand Staff's spaces and lines.

As children in our music classes, a lot of us were taught how to memorize the lines and spaces easily with the use of sentences. It does work especially for beginners who should always remember the names.

 For the Treble Clef Staff (upper staff), a simple sentence used to remember the names of the lines is: "Every Good Bird Does Fly." The first letter of each word of the sentence accurately names the five lines from the bottom of the staff to the top. That is, E G B D F.

To easily identify the names of the four spaces in the Treble Clef the simple word "FACE" can be used, the four different letters name the four spaces when read from the bottom to the top of the staff. That is, F A C E.

For the Bass Clef Staff (the bottom staff), a simple sentence used to remember the names of the lines is: "Good Boys Do Fine Always." The first letter of each word of the sentence accurately names the five lines of the Bass Clef Staff from the bottom to the top of the staff. That is, G B D F A.

The four spaces of the Bass Clef staff can be named by using the simple sentence, "All Cows Eat Grass". The first letter of each word of the sentence accurately names the four spaces of the Bass Clef Staff from the bottom to the top of the staff.

THE KEYBOARD

Using the piano keyboard as an example of wide ranged instruments, let us try to identify the pitches that go well with the note names assigned by the position of the notes on the Grand Staff as we have learned.

Just as in the Grand Staff, the music alphabets run from A through to G and then repeats over and over again in a sequence from left to right and right to left using the white keys on a piano key board.

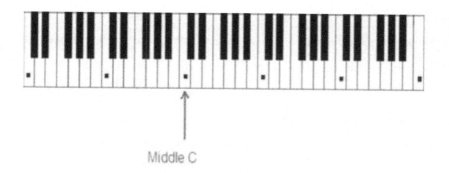

Middle C

The typical piano keyboard has 88 black and white keys altogether. The image above shows the exact location of the "Middle C", with this we can ascertain which lines and spaces represent different pitches played on the piano, or sung by a particular voice range or played on another instrument.

It is important to note that because the musical alphabet repeats over and over again, it is therefore helpful to allocate numbers to the complete set of letter for easy identification. For instance, to differentiate between a lower "A' from the higher "A", We make use of numbers to accompany the letter names, like "A3" so we know exactly where A3 should be located on both the keyboard and on the Grand Staff, and this will therefore help us know the exact pitch it will sound, whether high or low.

Since we now know for a fact that several notes on the keyboard and grand staff can share the same name (though not the same number), let us discuss the term 'Octave'

For the purpose of tis discourse, let us define the octave as the apparent distance between one note to the next note of the same name, this could be either left or right on the keyboard or up or down on the grand staff. When you sit in front of a piano and play an "A" on the keyboard, it will sound "compatible" when it played alongside another "A' whether an octave higher or lower, it will also, in fact, be "compatible" with any number of "A's" (the same thing will occur with any name or note that share the same name) played simultaneously on the keyboard. Whenever we play notes of the same name simultaneously, it will always produce a distinctive and compatible sound. This is what is known as playing the same notes on different octaves, What then is an Octave?

Piano Octaves

The first pianos were designed and constructed based on the layout of the harpsichord. The harpsichord had five octaves. Then the piano makers at that time increased to six octaves before they later increased to seven full octaves, this was done based on the request of piano players and composers at that time who needed a larger range when writing music for the piano. The standard piano with 88 keys was made in the late 1800s, adding about four keys to the outlay of the keyboard that we can recognize on any piano today.

The pattern of white and black keys we see on piano is repeated every 12 notes. This pattern includes five black keys and seven white keys. This is called an Octave. On the standard piano with 88 keys, there are about seven complete octaves plus a few other keys at both ends of the keyboard. If we consider an octave to begin at C, then there would be three keys in the zero octave at the lowest end of the keyboard, and one key in the last octave at the highest end.

While most modern pianos have 88 keys, there are many other practice keyboards with fewer keys than the seven full octaves. A shorter keyboard may only contain five to six octaves. However, there are also some piano makers that have increased the range of keys to 100 keys or more. In any case, the middle C note does not change, it sounds exactly the same, the difference in the octaves only occurs when notes are removed from either ends of the keyboard.

What then is the need to have a piano that has fewer or more keys than the standard 88 keys? Simple! If you desire to have a keyboard with which you can practice between your piano lesson schedules, but also with limited space, a shorter model gives you that chance to practice without taking up as much space as the standard piano. However, some piano pieces are written for a broader range than the standard outlay, this will require a piano with more than 88 keys.

There is however some speculation that pianos could have more keys than the current limit, but it comes at a cost both monetary cost, as well as the limitation of the limit of human hearing. With 88 keys, a piano is already close to the extent to which the human ear can hear. Adding more will increase the potential for more composition of music, yes but it will and may test the range of the human hearing. The standard 88-keys piano is just perfect for any kind of music you wish to make!

Back to our discussion on the piano keyboard and how they help identify notes and names of the lines and spaces on the great staff.

As beginner pianists, some of you already know the basics and elementary stuff about how the piano works. You may understand music and the different types of musical instruments we have, you may even understand the great staff and the different notes that make up the different lines and spaces. You may even go as far as understanding how the patterns of the black and white keys help in identifying the white keys. But one puzzling question you might have is, "why does the piano have white and black keys and not any other color combination". Well, I found myself asking the same question too when o started to learn the piano, hopefully, the next few paragraphs as we proceed will answer that question the way I was taught.

Okay! So the question is "why are black and white keys present on the piano? Well, the white keys actually represent the different musical tones and the black keys on the other hand represent half step intervals between the different musical tones. The black colored keys help pianists distinguish between the natural notes/pitches and the semitone notes/pitches. Is it making sense already? No? let us continue..

You are sure to ask another question say "why weren't other colors chosen?" because white and black keys look rather boring to the eye. Well, now take a brief moment and picture the piano with just white keys or just black keys, strange right?

You see how difficult it is to tell which key is A, G or even C? try telling which one is F# or G# or Eb, difficult yea? That's why it would be seemingly impossible to assign notes to the keys of the piano if they were all just white keys or all black keys. The white and black keys both have their distinct functions and it helps making music more fun.

The black keys actually help to separate the white notes from one other in a rather sequential pattern. With this, the black keys not only help you determine an A from a middle C for instance, but they also help to know which octave range you're playing in.

Also, the materials used in making the different notes come to play too. Earlier on, I asked why the piano keys came in white and black and not other colors, like red, blue and the likes, well not that they cannot come in different colors other than white or black, you could as well just paint them whatever colors you want and even decide to make beautiful rainbow patterns out of them, it would be fun yea? Well, going by history and how the first pianos came to be, the piano keys were built with two main materials, which were ivory and ebony.

The white keys were made from ivory hence, its natural white color because ivory is actually a bright colored material. The black keys on the other hand were made from ebony, with ebony being a natural dark colored material, hence, the dark color of the black keys. Funny that there exist some pianos where the keys are actually reversed, meaning the white keys would be black keys and the black keys as white keys.

However, as pianist in training and as pianists generally, the less we worry about the color scheme of the keyboard the better. Looking at the keyboard, it's much easier and appealing to the eyes the way the keys are colored black and white. Actually, we use the black keys as guides as we play through different musical pieces. It is not only appealing visually, but also physically.

The manner in which the keys are arranged makes it easy for the fingers to just flow as it plays the keyboard. The smooth contours also help pianists and players play as naturally as they can and not have any difficulty sort of, the pattern is a blessing! Now you would agree that if there were no black keys, we are sure to have a lot of hard time playing anything at all.

As I stated earlier, the white and black keys used to be reversed. If you've ever seen up pictures of older keyboard instruments before now, you might have noticed that the black and white key colors were reversed. Example is the harpsichord and the earlier models of the fortepiano, the white natural keys were indeed black!. While the half steps that are now black were white.

So why then exactly did they switch the colors of the keys to the way they are now? Well, the answer actually takes us back to what I talked about earlier. It was just too difficult to identify the colors and the key colors ended up blending in with themselves. With the black keys particularly, the little dark space in between them made it really hard to see, so it was very easy to make mistakes while playing those instruments.

However, on a modern piano, the spaces between the white keys are easier to tell, the dark line between each white keys so we can tell one from the other. The relative distance between the keys is apparent, when playing octaves especially.

NATURALS, FLATS AND SHARPS

The white keys of the keyboard are often known as naturals; it basically means that the notes are in their natural-sounding state. It is there that the notes have their original sound, free of accidentals and changes. So Instead of just calling those notes as just C or D, you add the word natural at the end. From a theoretical point of view, it makes sense and it helps in describing music to others.

For the black keys of the keyboard, we normally call them sharps and flats. The black keys actually help the white keys reach a state of change asides from just sounding natural. What happens is really fun and interesting at least to me and it should be to you too. Take a natural note and analyze the position of the black key in relation to it.

For instance, locate 'A' natural and then look at the first black key directly above it in front. That key is a higher tone (half a step up) so we call that note A sharp!

What about the black note that is directly below it behind? When you play that note, you'd discover that it actually sounds lower that the A natural note. (in this case, you are playing a half step down). We call this note an A flat. Now still imagine if we had all white keys, we are sure to have a tougher time trying to know which note is which, well except you have an excellent ear to decode the actual pitch.

How many black and white keys are on the piano?

Another interesting question you might want to ask is, how many keys are there really on the piano? If you don't know, here is an answer for you. As you know already, a full size standard keyboard has 88 keys. And if you're still wondering how many black and white keys there are, there are 36 black keys, well it seems like a lot but alternatively, there are 52 white keys, altogether making up the 88 keys of the standard piano!

The piano is divided up into a series of repetitive patterns that we call octaves. In total there are 7 octaves for the standard keyboard. That is, for every 7 white keys, you have 5 black keys that help you break down patterns of the tones. These 7 notes actually make up a scale.

Whether you want to play a major or minor scale, it has to be broken up by a certain pattern of whole and half steps in order to sound right. And 5 black keys is just enough to give you what you need to compliment the white keys and give you what you need to create different modes of scales.

Why Do Pianos Have 88 Keys?

So now we know about octaves and the different amounts of keys, but why do pianos have 88 keys? It could have been 100 or even more, why is it 88? Well, the answer to that question is pretty simple but would require we go back in time to history.

Back in the days before now, pianists played an instrument that didn't have as many keys as the piano. It was called the harpsichord, it had only about a total of 60 keys.

As music evolved and modernized, the harpsichord wasn't doing enough to meet the standard of music produced. Because if you take a very good look at the music at was composed and produced at that time and even up to this day, no composer actually goes beyond the 7 octaves that a standard piano has. When we consider the pitches of the modern piano these days. The higher you go in pitch, the tougher it is for someone to hear; especially old people. The same applies to lower range, it becomes more difficult to detect pitches when it's at low frequency. Steinway (the American company that makes pianos) set the trend with the 88 key models and ever since it has been a standard for other piano makers to imitate.

After that, things started to pop up in the right way. First, there are both black and white keys, second, there is a sequential pattern the keys on piano repeat themselves. Although, while many modern pianos contain 88 keys, we find those with a shorter range of keys and even those with increased number, up to a 100!

Black and White Keys on Piano

Now we know that pianos are arranged with white keys with the musical tones of A , B , C , D , E , F, and G. While the black keys only fill in the gaps for the remaining half-steps, these half steps are noted as flats or sharps as key signatures or accidentals when writing music for the piano.

As often as you practice scales, you'd get familiar with the keys and notes on the keyboard, but to start with. The C scale, for instance, is played without accidentals, that is without any flats or sharps. Meaning that all the notes are played exclusively on the white keys. However, other musical scales may include one or more of the black keys, depending on how many flats and sharps the key has. For example, the key D has two sharps in it, which are F sharp and C sharp, and both are played using the black keys.

ACCIDENTALS

An accidental is a note among the notes of a pitch that is not among the scale. In music, the sharp (♯) , flat (♭), natural (♮) symbols, among others, are examples of such notes, and those notes are also called accidentals.

In any given bar on the grand staff where it appears, an accidental sign means that the following note(and anywhere that note appears on the entire staff) will be raised or lowered from its natural pitch, regardless of the key signature. Usually, a note is raised or lowered by one semitone, and there are also double sharps or double flats, which in cases where they appear raise or lower the note by two semitones. As I mentioned earlier, accidentals apply to any note as well as anywhere the note repeat on the entire staff, unless they are canceled by another accidental sign.

The modern accidental signs were derived from the two forms of small letter "b" used in the Gregorian chant manuscripts long ago to signify the two different pitches of "B", the only note that could be changed at that time. The "round" b turned out to become the flat sign, while the "square" b became the natural and sharp signs.

The black keys on the piano keyboard are sometimes called "accidentals" or sharps most times, while the white keys are also called naturals.

Order Of Sharps And Flats

We already know that sharps raise the natural notes by half a tone and flats on the other hand lower the natural notes by half a tone. They actually perform similar tasks but they work in opposite directions. Similarly, when we try to learn the order of flats and sharps, we'll discover that they are also opposites of each other.

Before we take a look at ways to remember the order of the sharps and flats, let's consider how they are arranged, shall we?

Flats and sharps in the Major Key

KEY	NUMBER OF SHARPS	KEY	NUMBR OF FLATS
C MAJOR	-	-	-
G MAJOR	1	F MAJOR	1
D MAJOR	2	B FLAT MAJOR	2
A MAJOR	3	E FLAT MAJOR	3
E MAJOR	4	A FLAT MAJOR	4
B MAJOR	5	D FLAT MAJOR	5
F SHARP MAOR	6	G SHARP MAJOR	6
C SHARP MAJOR	7	C FLAT MAJOR	7

Let us start with the sharps, to know the number of sharps of each key, we will work with the number 5. Have it in mind, the number 5. As long as you remember the number 5, mastering the flats and sharps will be easy.

From the table, C major neither has zero sharps.

Now to find the first key that has the first sharp in it, we simply count five notes from C, we count up from C (also remember that the sharps raise a note). Let's count up from C, C is 1, then D is 2, E is 3 F is 4, and G is 5! Our fifth count falls on G, meaning that G is the first key with a sharp in it. As we can see form the table, G major has one sharp note and that sharp is on the key F, because that's the key directly below G. meaning the sharp key for G major is **(F #)**

Now let's find the next note with two sharps. We count five from G, G is 1, then A is 2, B is 3, C is 4 and D is 5! D is the note with two sharps as we can see from the table that D major has 2 sharps. The two sharps falls on the key F(because that's the first sharp key) and key C, because that's the note directly below D. meaning the sharp keys for D major are **(F # and C #)**

Now let's find the next note with three sharps. We count five from D, D is 1, then E is 2, F is 3, G is 4 and A is 5! A is the note with three sharps as we can see from the table that A major has 3 sharps. The three sharps falls on the key F, key C and key G (because G is the note directly below A). meaning the sharp keys for D major are **(F #, C # and G #).**

Now let's find the next note with four sharps. We count five from A, A is 1, then B is 2, C is 3, D is 4 and E is 5! E is the note with four sharps as we can see from the table that E major has 4 sharps. The four sharps falls on the key F, key C, key G and key D (because D is the note directly below E). meaning the sharp keys for E major are **(F #, C #, G # and D #).**

Now let's find the next note with five sharps. We count five from E, E is 1, then F is 2, G is 3, A is 4 and B is 5! B is the note with five sharps as we can see from the table that B major has 5 sharps. The five sharps falls on the key F, key C, key G, key D and key A (because A is the note directly below B). meaning the sharp keys for B major are **(F #, C #, G #, D # and A #).**

Now let's find the next note with six sharps. We count five from B, B is 1, then C is 2, D is 3, E is 4 and F is 5! F is the note with six sharps as we can see from the table that F major has 6 sharps. The six sharps falls on key F, key C, key G, key D, key A and key E (because E is the note directly below F). meaning the sharp keys for F major are **(F #, C #, G #, D #, A # and E #).**

Now let's find the next note with seven sharps. We count five from F, F is 1, then G is 2, A is 3, B is 4 and C is 5! C is the note with seven sharps as we can see from the table that C major has 7 sharps. The seven sharps falls on key F, key C, key G, key D, key A, key E and key B (because B is the note directly below C). meaning the sharp keys for C major are **(F #, C #, G #, D #, A #, E # and B #).**

Pretty simple yea? From our little exercise, sharp keys are simply ordered in 5 notes up from each other, the final sharp falls on the note directly below the ultimate note, this is also called the leading note.

Now let us do that of the flats. The pattern is pretty much the same as with the sharps. We work with the number 5 again.

As we know, flats work in the opposite direction as the sharps. While the sharps raise a note by half a tone, the flats lower a note by half a tone. While we counted 5 notes above for the sharps, we would be counting 5 notes below for the flats. (Remember, sharps raise a note while flats lower a note)

From our table, C major has zero flats.

Now to find the key with the first flat, we count 5 notes below C (remember that flats lower a note). We count from C, C is 1, B is 2, A is 3, G is 4 and F is 5! Our fifth note is F, from our table, F major is the first key with one flat. The flat falls on the key B (because B is the note directly below C) Meaning the flat key for F major is **(B ♭)**

Now to find the key with two flats, we count 5 notes below F (remember that flats lower a note). We count from F, F is 1, E is 2, D is 3, C is 4 and B is 5! Our fifth note is B, from our table, B flat major is the key with two flats in it. The flat keys falls on the key B. what do you think the second one is? We count down with one note from

F(the note with the first flat) and we get E. Meaning the flat keys for B major are **(B ♭ and E ♭)**

To find the key with three flats, we count 5 notes below B (remember that flats lower a note). We count from B, B is 1, A is 2, G is 3, F is 4 and E is 5! Our fifth note is E, from our table, E flat major is the key with three flats in it. The flat keys falls on the key B and key E. what do you think the third one is? Like we did for B, We count down with one note from B(the note with two flats) and we get A. Meaning the flat keys for E flat major are **(B ♭ , E ♭ and A ♭)**

To find the key with four flats, we count 5 notes below E (remember that flats lower a note). We count from E, E is 1, D is 2, C is 3, B is 4 and A is 5! Our fifth note is A, from our table, A flat major is the key with four flats in it. The flat keys falls on the key B, key E, key A, what do you think the fourth one is? Like we did for E, We count down with one note from E(the note with three flats) and we get D. Meaning the flat keys for A flat major are **(B ♭ , E ♭ , A ♭ and D ♭)**

To find the key with five flats, we count 5 notes below A (remember that flats lower a note). We count from A, A is 1, G is 2, F is 3, E is 4 and D is 5! Our fifth note is D, from our table, D flat major is the key with five flats in it. The flat keys falls on the key B, key E, key A, key D, what do you think the fifth one is? Like we did for A, We count down with one note from A(the note with four flats) and we get G. Meaning the flat keys for D flat major are **(B ♭ , E ♭ , A ♭ , D ♭ and G ♭)**

To find the key with six flats, we count 5 notes below D (remember that flats lower a note). We count from D, D is 1, C is 2, B is 3, A is 4 and G is 5! Our fifth note is G, from our table, G flat major is the key with six flats in it. The flat keys falls on the key B, key E, key A, key D, key G, what do you think the sixth one is? Like we did for D, We count down with one note from D (the note with five flats) and we get C. Meaning the flat keys for G flat major are **(B ♭ , E ♭ , A ♭ , D ♭ , G ♭ and C ♭)**

To find the key with seven flats, we count 5 notes below G (remember that flats lower a note). We count from G, G is 1, F is 2, E is 3, D is 4 and C is 5! Our fifth note is C, from our table, C flat major is the key with seven flats in it. The flat keys falls on the key B, key E, key A, key D, key G, key C, what do you think the seventh one is? Like we did for G, We count down with one note from G (the note with six flats) and we get F. Meaning the flat keys for C flat major are **(B ♭ , E ♭ , A ♭ , D ♭ , G ♭ , C ♭ and F ♭)**

This pattern forms an order we call the order of Sharps and Flats.

The Order of Sharps and the Order of Flats

When we talk about the circle of fifths, there we will learn that every key has a specific number of flats and sharps. The sharps and flats for each key are not that random and like we learned, they follow a specific order that you need to keep at heart and memorize so you can always remember. We call this order the 'Order of flats and sharps'.

After memorizing the order of flats and sharps in relation to the number of flats and sharps in each key, you should be able to spell the notes for each key. Because when you start playing the piano, you will always play in some key, therefore knowing your keys and how they are arranged will help you a great deal.

The Order of Sharps

The order of sharps is:F #C #G #D #A #E #B #

The order of sharps is similar to the order of flats

As we know, the G major key has only 1 sharp and that sharp has to be the first on the order of sharps, that is, F #. So when we write out the G major scale, it looks like this: G, A, B, C, D, E, and F #.

In A major, there are three sharps, meaning those sharps would be the first three sharps from the order, that is, F #, C #, and G #. So when we write out the scale of A major, it looks like this: A, B, C #, D, E, F #, and G #.

When we work with key signatures that involves the order of sharps, the sharps always occur in a particular pattern and order. And a good way to always remember this order is when we use the letters of the order of sharps to form a sentence, **Father Charles Goes Down And Ends Battle**. So that when you have a music scale with one sharp, that sharp is always "Father" or (F sharp). A scale with two sharps in it would be "Father and Charles" or (F sharp) and (C sharp). The key signature or scale with three sharps would be "Father, Charles and Goes" or (F sharp) (C sharp) and (G sharp) and so on till the end.

The order of Flats

The order of flats:B bE bA bD bG bC bF b

The order of flats contains the names of seven flat notes. The order simply tells you the notes that are flat in a key that contains flats. For instance, if a key has one flat, it means the key contains the first flat in the order of flats, that is B b. In the cases where the key has two flats, it will contain the first and the second flats from the order of flats, that is B b and E b. The key with 5 flats as we now know will contain the first 5 flats from the order of flats, that is B b, E b, A b, D b, and G b.

The key F has only 1 flat, meaning the flat must be the first flat which is B b. So that when we write out the scale of F, all the other letter names will be natural notes with the inclusion of B b. This is how it looks like, F, G, A, B b, C, D, E.! There, the scale of F, because F has one flat note from our order of flats and that flat note is B b.

Let's take another example, from our order of flats, key A b major contains 4 flat notes. That means it would take up the first 4 flats in our order of flats, that is, B b, E b, A b, and D b. This is how it looks like, A b, B b, C, D b, E b, F, G! There, the scale of A b, because A b has four flat notes from our order of flats and those flat notes are B b, E b, A b and D b.

As with the order of sharps, when working with key signatures that involves the order of flats, the flats also occur in a particular order or pattern. And to remember this order, we simply take the sentence we formed with the order of sharps, you remember "Father Charles Goes Down And Ends Battle", all we do is say it backwards in order to remember the order of flats, let's try it: **"Battle Ends And Down Goes Charles' Father"**. Just like with the sharp scales, if you have any scale with one flat, it would be "Battle" or (B flat). A scale with Two flats would be "Battle and Ends" or (B flat) and (E flat) and so on till the end.

How to memorize the Order of Flats and Sharps.

Certain people just prefer to memorize the order of sharps and flats rather engage in that mathematics we did earlier. All the same, just in case you forget the technique, here's a little trick to help you always remember the order of sharps and flats. First let us outline the order of sharps and flats;

SHARPS: F C G D A E B

FLATS: B E A D G C F

When you look at it closely, you'll find a pattern, the sharps are more like the opposite of the flats. The letters are a mirror image of themselves, so if you can memorize one of them, to remember the other just invert it. However, the diagram below combines the method we used and just makes it easier for you to remember.

Sharp Keys Graph:

Key	Sharps	Number of sharps
G	F #	1
D	F #, C #	2
A	F #, C #, G #	3
E	F #, C #, G #. D #	4
B	F #, C #, G #, D #, A #	5
F#	F #, C #, G #, D #,	6

	A #, E #	
C#	F #, C #, G #, D #, A #, E #, B#	7

Flat Keys Graph:

Key	Flats	Number of flats
F	B ♭	1
B ♭	B ♭ , E ♭	2
E ♭	B ♭ , E ♭ , A ♭	3
A ♭	B ♭ , E ♭ , A ♭ , D ♭	4
G ♭	B ♭ , E ♭ , A ♭ , D ♭ , G ♭	5
D ♭	B ♭ , E ♭ , A ♭ , D ♭ , G ♭ , C ♭	6
C ♭	B ♭ , E ♭ , A ♭ , D ♭ , G ♭ , C ♭ , F ♭	7

HOW TO MEMORIZE THE ORDER OF FLATS AND SHARPS

What you need to do to remember the order of flats is to keep in mind the word B E A D plus three other letters G C F. While the order of sharps is pretty much the same only that it is reversed, that is, F C G D A E B.

Or like we did earlier with using sentences to remember, because some people prefer the use of sentences but either ways, both are still classic memory aids to help you remember the order of flats and sharps.

For the order of flats, we have: Battle Ends And Down Goes Charles' Father

Battle	**Ends**	**And**	**Down**	**Goes**	**Charles'**	**Father**
B ♭ major	E ♭ major	A ♭ major	D ♭ major	G ♭ major	C major	F major
2 flats	3 flats	4 flats	5 flats	6 flats	0 flats	1 flat
					C ♭ major (7 flats)	

While for the order of sharps, we have: Father Charles Goes Down And Ends Battle

Father	**Charles**	**Goes**	**Down**	**And**	**Ends**	**Battle**
F# major	C major	G major	D major	A major	E major	B maor
6 sharps	0 sharps	1 sharp	2 sharps	3 sharps	4 harps	5 sharps
	C# major (7 sharps)					

You can memorize with either or both methods to help you on your way to becoming a good piano player.

HOW KEY SIGNATURES USE THE ORDER OF FLATS AND SHARPS

When you look at the circle of fifths diagram, there you will see that I included all the fifiteen key signatures used in music, you will also notice that all the sharps and flats are written in the right order as we learnt.

 One funny question beginners ask is, "Why Do We Need Notes Like A b, F b, C #, and B #?"

Some students are most times confused why the inclusion of notes like that are necessary, to them isn't C b the same as B, and F b the same as E? Well, here's the reason why

When we write out scales for notes, we try not to sip letters and we tey as much as possible to avoid having two same letters occurring in the same scale, like B and B b. You would agree that it would make reading music a bit difficult.

Here is an example of how funny a scale will look like when it is improperly spelt, let's take the key of G b major, it could be could be improperly written as: G b, A b, B b, B, D b, E b, and F. Did you notice that there are two B notes and no C note? But when it is properly written out, it looks like this: G b, A b, B b, C, D b, E b, and F.

The Circle Of Fifths

Many people use the circle of fifths to understand how sharps and flats work, they use the circle of fifths anytime they want to figure out which note's scales have which key signatures. The Circle of fifth is simply the way the key signatures of scales are arranged and organized. It works with a very simple principle as we have learnt before called the 'interval of the perfect fifth'. That is one key signature is at an interval away from the next one with a perfect fifth count. For instance, as we know that the C major scale has no sharps nor flats, so moving up by a perfect fifth will help us find the scale with one sharp in it, which is G, as we learnt. And if you go up by another perfect fifth, you will find the scale wit two sharps in it,that is, D. the same thing goes for the flats scales too, starting at C major, when you go down a perfect fifth, you will find the first scale with a flat, and that is F. and of you go down by another perfect fifth, you will find the note with two flats in it, that is, B. and so on till the end.

Here is a diagram of how the circle of fifth looks like;

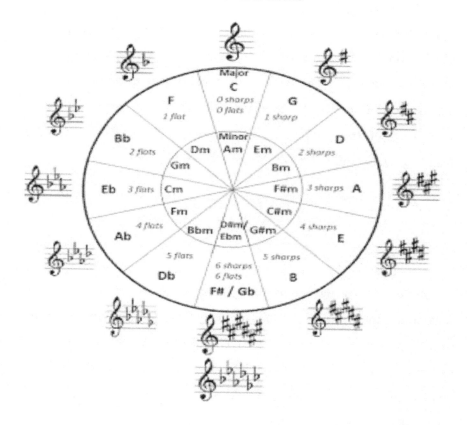

MEMORIZING THE CIRCLE OF FIFTHS

Many musicians and piano players just prefer to memorize the key signatures because the cirle of fifths looks rather complicated. But to help you with the major key signatures, all you have to do is remember that sentences we formed, "Father Charles...", remember? And also remember that the C major scale has zero flats and sharps.

Now start counting your sharps from C, that is "Charles", which represents zero sharps for C major. As you continue add one sharp as you go through the words until you come back to Charles again, which represents C# major(C sharp major) and its seven sharps (that is, C(zero sharps), D (1 sharp), E (2 sharps), F (three sharps), G (four sharps), A (five sharps), B (six sharps) and back to C (seven sharps)—To further help you, you can say that "C is all and nothing". That is, C sharp major has all the sharps and C major has nothing.

We can also use the same trick for the flats too.

Those extra sharps written in minor scale pieces are called accidentals, meaning, they don't originally belong in the key signature of the notes. Now to find the relative minor keys for any major key, we simply count the scale down three semitones. We know that the relative minor key to C Major is A Minor, so we can work out any other relative minor using the same process.

For instance, when we count three semitones from the G major key, we get to E, that is, E is the relative minor of G Major, meaning they both share the same key signature of one sharp. Also when we raise the leading note to make the harmony sound right, we will have D sharps in the music.

Key Signature

A key signature is the symbol at the beginning of a song piece that tells us which piano notes should be sharp or flat for the entire the song, even more, the key signature tells us which scale the notes of the song was written.

E-flat major scale

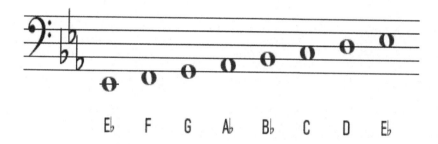

From the above example, we see that every B, E and A in the piece will be flat. Meaning that, the scale has 3 flats (B ♭ , E ♭ and A ♭) and of course we know that the key with three flats in it is E ♭ (E flat) major. The key signature therefore tells us that this particular song was composed using the notes of the E ♭ (E flat) major scale. How interesting! Now you see why learning the scales was in fact, a good idea.

Why is it important to know the Key Signature for a song?

The key signature not only helps you understand which notes are to be sharpened or flattened, they also give you a hint to which chords you are likely to encounter while playing a piece on a particular key. The same way a certain number of flats and sharps are associated with different keys, so are chords associated with different keys too. Our typical example, the C major scale that has no sharps or flats in it, when you play chords with the C major key, the chords won't have flats or sharps either.

Where does the Key Signature come from?

A major scale is built on a pattern of tones (T) and semitones (S), that's why it sounds the way it does. Like I said, it operates like a pattern and if you follow the pattern, any scale you create will sound like a major scale. A semitone is the smallest space between one note and the next. On the piano, the semitone is the space between one note to the next (either a black or a white key). A tone is two semitones joined together. Here is how the C major scale looks like on the piano:

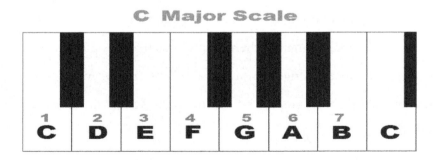

Key Signature Rules

Here are a few key signature rules to guide us:

- There can be only one major scale for every key signature.

- Major scales never use flats and sharps together, it's either one of them.

- The highest number of sharps or flats you can have on a scale is 7.

- The order of flats and sharps follows a specific pattern/order and it never changes.

- The sharps and flats are always written on specific lines and spaces when writing key signatures on the grand staff.

Minor Key Signatures?

Now let us examine the sharp and flats of minor keys. Yes! The first one we examined were for the major keys, I'm sure the question on your mind is "What is the difference between major and minor keys?" That question will be answered very soon.

Minor keys in relation to major keys take their key signatures (we'll discuss key signatures in subsequent sections) from the major keys they're related to. Therefore, we call those minor keys "relative" minors, because they take up the key signature and some of the notes from the major keys they are related to.

For instance, A minor and C Major are both relative. Meaning that the key signatures for C major will be the same in A minor, and we know that C major has no sharps nor flats, A minor will therefore have no sharps nor flats.

A lot of the music we listen to use the minor scale in its harmonic form. Meaning that the scale provides harmony and melody. Like we discussed in the previous subchapter, the seventh note in the major scale is called the leading note, just like in the case of B in the C major scale. The leading note, B is just one semitone below C, meaning there are no white or black notes between them. Therefore, to make music using minor keys like with the major keys, we would raise the leading note to create a semitone between the seventh and eighth notes of the scale. That easy!

Let us take an example, in the key of A Minor for instance, the leading note is G, because it is one semitone lower than A. When you start to really play the piano, and play in the A minor key, you're likely to notice lots of G sharps in the piece

Let me make it clear here that not all songs are written in the major scale. Most sad songs you hear were probably written using the minor scale or using the key signature of a minor scale.. However, you do not have to learn a whole new set of key signatures for the minor scales. The minor scales only take up the key signatures of a relative major scale.

Rules:

- Every major key signature has a minor scale with which they share key signatures.
- These major/minor pairs are called "relative" majors/minors because they share the same notes/key signatures.
- To find the key signature of a minor scale, you go 3 semitones up to find the relative major.

THE KEY SIGNATURE CHART

The key signature charts below are for both Sharp Major Scales and Flat Major Scales. Using the charts will help you identify major Scale Key Signatures as you progress in your journey to being a good piano payer.

The sharp Major Scale Key Signatures Chart

KEY SIGNATURESNUMBER OF SHARPSSHARPENED NOTESMINOR KEYSENHARMONIC

C major0NoneA minorNone

G major1F E minorNone

D major2F C B minorNone

A major3F C G F ♯ minorNone

E major4F C G D C ♯ minorNone

B major5 F C G D A G ♯ minor C ♭ major & A ♭ minor

F ♯ major6F C G D A E D ♯ minor G ♭ major & E ♭ minor

C ♯ major7F C G D A E D A ♯ minor D ♭ major & B ♭ minor

The flat Major Scale Key Signatures Chart

KEY SIGNATURES NUMBER OF FLATSFLATTENED NOTESMINOR KEYSENHARMONIC

C major0None A minorNone

F major1B D minorNone

B ♭ major2B E G minorNone

E ♭ major3B E A C minorNone

A ♭ major4B E A D F minorNone

D ♭ major5B E A D G B ♭ minor C ♯ major & A ♯ minor

G ♭ major6B E A D G C E ♭ minor F ♯ major & D ♯ minor

C ♭ major7B E A D G C F A ♭ minor B major & G♯ minor

The Note Family: Signs And Symbols

In music, the Italian word "tempo," is used to mean "time," and it refers to the speed of a piece of music or a composition. The time or tempo is measured in BPM, beats per minute. For example, 50BPM tempo means 50 beats in one minute, approximately one beat every second. Whereas, a 120BPM tempo would mean 120 beats in one minute, or better still two beats per second. Simply put, the higher the value, the faster the tempo!

When you look at some musical pieces, you will find italian words like tempo, allegro, moderato, adante and several others. All of them simply indicate the speed of a rhythm. However, they all have their disparate meanings, for instance, the word 'presto' means 'quick' and by quick it means that any speed not lower than 170BPM is just fine. We will learn more about tempo when we discuss time signatures, rests and measures.

For now, let's take a peek at the note family; their signs and symbols.

QUARTER NOTES OR CROTCHETS

crotchet

In music, the duration of sound is represented by a symbol. These symbols that are used to represent duration of sounds are known as Note Values. In Britain, the name used for each note value on the grand staff is the Crotchet, while in America, it is called the Quarter note.

The note symbol for the crotchet is formed by a thin vertical line called the 'stem' and an oval shaped head called the 'notehead', or simply 'head'. On the staff, the apparent position of the notehead signifies the musical note or the pitch. On the grand staff, if the notehead is above the third line, the stem will be positioned downwards and to the left hand side of the notehead. Also, If the notehead is below the third line on the grand staff, the stem will be positioned upward facing the right hand side of the notehead.

EIGHTH NOTES OR QUAVERS

quaver

In America, the name of this symbol is the eighth note, while in Britain, the name of this symbol is the quaver. Being the eight note, it lasts half of the quarter note ($1/2 \times 1/4 = 1/8$). To complete one beat, we need two quavers. When you look at quaver notes closely, what striking difference do you see? If you saw it right, it is the horizontal line that groups the notes. That horizontal line is called a 'beam'. There's nothing technical about the beam, it just helps us to identify the quavers as different from the other notes. Without the notes, this is how they would look like:

That symbol that replaces the beam is called a flag. However, the sound doesn't change whether the beams or flags are used, like I said earlier, it's about identifying the quavers easily. But anytime the eighth notes are placed in one or two beats, the beam should be used and not the flags.

SIXTEENTH NOTES OR SEMIQUAVERS

In America, the name of this note is the sixteenth note, while the British name is called the Semiquaver. The Sixteenth notes or semiquavers lasts half of the eighth note (1/2x1/8=1/16). To complete a beat, we need four sixteenth notes. Just like the quavers, when you look closely at the semiquavers, the striking difference in appearance is the use of a double line or double beam when they are grouped together. And when they are not grouped together, they use two flags.

THIRTY-SECOND NOTES OR DEMISEMIQUAVERS

This new note is called the Thirty-second notes in America and the "Demisemiquavers" in Britain. The Demisemiquavers or thirty-second note lasts half the sixteenth note(1/2x1/16=1/32). When in groups, the demisemiquavers use a triple beam and when they are not grouped, they use three flags. To complete a beat, we need eight demisemiquavers.

SIXTY-FOURTH NOTE OR HEMIDEMISEMIQUAVER

As you must have noticed already, every new symbol lasts half of the previous symbol. Thus new symbol follows the same pattern, the sixty-fourth note or Hemidemisemiquaver lasts half of the thirty-second note $(1/2x1/32=1/64)$ To complete a beat, we need sixteen hemideisemiquavers.

MINIMS AND SEMIBREVES

minim

These new note symbols are called half notes or minims. When you look at it closely, the difference between the half note note and the quarter note is that the head of the half note is empty. The m=half notes or minims represents a double quarter note, meaning it lasts for two beats.

The semibreve or whole note lasts for four beats, and it is different from the others because it does not have a stem:

semibreve

As a way to summarize the note symbols and what they mean, the American name given to each note symbol is simply the duration of the note in relation to the whole note or semibreve. For instance, the half note or minim is half a whole note, meaning we need two half notes to make up the duration of a whole note. Similarly, the quarter note or crotchet is a fourth of the whole note, so to complete the duration of the whole note, we would need four quarter notes or crotchets.

Time signatures.

The time signature is also known as the meter signature or measure signature. It is a notational phrase used in most Western musical notation, the function in any musical piece is to indicate how many pulses or beats should be contained in every measure or bar, and it also indicates which note value (minim, semibreve, crotchet...) is equivalent to one beat.

In a typical musical score, the time signature or the meter signature is located at the beginning of the staff as a symbol of stacked numbers, usually one number on top of the other. The numbers could be 3 on top of four, or 4 on top of 4. The time signature usually follows the key signature immediately or following the clef symbol immediately in cases where the key signature is empty.

A time signature known as the mid-score , usually follows immediately after a barline, and it signifies a change of meter.

In music notation, there are several types of time signatures, although, the various types is dependent on whether the musical piece follows a symmetrical or regular beat pattern. The types of time signatures includes

Simple time signatures for example (3 4 beat and 4 4 beat; it's pronounced, three four beat and four four beat)

Compound time signature, for example (9 8 beat and 12 8 beat; pronounced as, nine eight beat and twelve eight beat)

Or in cases where the musical piece involves shifting beat patterns, the time signature may be complex, for example (5 4 beat or 7 8 beat; pronounced as five four beat or seven eight beat),

Mixed time signature, for example; (5 8 beat and 3 8 beat, pronounced as five eight beat or three eight beat) or (6 8 and 3 4; pronounced six eight beat and three four beat)

Additive time signature, for instance (3+2+3 8 beat; pronounced as three plus two plus three eight beat)

Fractional time signature, for example (2 1/2 4 beat; pronounced as two and a half four beat)

Irrational time signatures, for example (3 10 or 5 24; pronounced as three ten beat or five twenty four beat)

Whenever you find these numbers on a musical staff or piece, they indicate the number of beats that are within each bar of the musical piece, they are more like beat guides when you play a piece. Let's take a look at the most frequently used time signatures and what they stand for!

FREQUENTLY USED TIME SIGNATURES

The basic time signatures include the;

- 4 4 beat (four four beat). It is also known as the common time.

- 2 2 beat (two two beat) also known as alla breve or cut time or cut-common time

- 2 4 beat (two four beat) and 3 4 beat (three four beat) are known as simple time signatures

- The 6 8 beat (six eight beat) is known as the compound time signatures

SIMPLE TIME SIGNATURE

The simple time signatures usually consist of two numbers, one above the other:

$$\frac{2}{4} \qquad \frac{3}{4} \qquad \frac{4}{4}$$

The lower number signifies the note value representing one beat or the beat unit. The lower number is usually at a power of 2.

The upper number tells us how many such beats (the value of the lower number) should be played in a given bar.

For example;

 2 4 beat simply means two quarter-notes or two crotchet beats per bar

3 8 beat means three eighth-note or three quaver beats per bar.

Easy yea?

The most common simple time signatures used are the 2 4 beat (two four beat), 3 4 beat (three four beat), and 4 4 beat (four four beat).

Conventionally, two symbols are specially used for the 4 4 beat (four four beat) and the 2 2 beat (two two beat):

The symbol is however, sometimes used for 4 4 beat (four four beat) also called the imperfect time or the compound time. As it looks, the symbol is gotten from a broken circle which was used in music notation in the 14th century through to the 16th century, where a full circle represented what would be written today in the 3 2 beat (three two beat) or 3 4 beat (three four beat) and was called perfect time (tempus perfectum)

The symbol was also brought down from the music notational practice of the Renaissance and late- Medieval music era music, where it indicated a diminished imperfect time (tempus imperfectum diminutum) or more precisely, double speed or proportio dupla, in the duple meter. However, in modern music notation, the symbol is used in place of the 2 2 beat (two two beat) also known as alla breve or colloquially, cut common time or cut time.

COMPOUND TIME SIGNATURE

In compound time signatures, the upper numbers represent what we call subdivisions, these subdivisions are divided into three equal parts, so that a dotted note, that is, a note half longer than a regular note becomes the beat. The upper numbers of a compound time signature is usually 3, 6, 9, or 12 (which are all multiples of 3 in each beat), while the lower number is usually an 8 (a quaver note or an eight note), as in 9 8 beat (nine eight beat) or 12 8 beat (twelve eight beat).

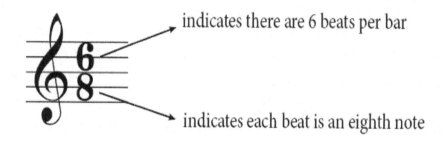

indicates there are 6 beats per bar

indicates each beat is an eighth note

Simple: 3 4 beat (three four beat) is an example of a simple triple meter time signature that denotes three quarter notes or three crotchet beats. It is played as "one and two and three and ..."(you can count it out loud or tap a table or clap your hands to practice the beat)

Compound: As a principle, 6 8 beat (six eight beat) consists not of three different groups of two eighth notes or quaver notes but two groups of three eighth-note or quaver subdivisions. It is played as "one two three four five six ..." (You can count it out loud or tap a table or clap your hands to practice the beat)

The example of the compound time signature sated above assumes that continuous eighth notes or quaver notes are the most occurring note values. However, the rhythm of an actual music is not always that regular.

Time signatures that indicate two beats per bar whether in a simple or compound meter are called duple meter, while those that have three beats per bar are called triple meter. Other terms like quadruple (4), quintuple (5), and the likes, are also used occasionally.

BEAT IN TIME SIGNATURES.

To the human ear, a bar may sound like a single beat. For example, in a fast waltz music, written in the 3 4 time (three four time), the time signature may be described as being one in a bar. Similarly, at slower tempos than fast music, the beat notated by the time signature could be subdivided into smaller units in an actual performance.

From the understanding of mathematics, time signatures like the 3 4 beat (three four beat) and the 3 8 beat (three eight beat) can be interchanged. Meaning, all the simple triple time signatures, such as the 3 8 beat (three eight beat), 3 4 beat (three four beat), 3 2 beat (three two beat), etc. and all the compound duple time signatures, such as the 6 8 beat (six eight beat), 6 16 beat (six sixteen beat) and many more can be considered as equivalent.

In a sense, a musical piece originally written in the 3 4 time (three four time) can simply be rewritten in the 3 8 time (three eight time), this could be achieved by reducing the length of the notes by half!.

It's also possible to rewrite other time signatures too, in most cases a simple time signature with triplets can translate into a compound meter.

Although, a time signature can be formally interchanged for a performing musician or composer, conventionally, different time signatures usually have different meanings and connotations. Firstly, in a beat, a smaller note value usually implies a more compound or complex notation, and this can affect the ease of the musical performance. Secondly, something we call beaming can affect the choice of an actual beat division. For example, it is more natural to use the crotchet or quarter note as a beat unit in the 6 4 time (six four time) or in the 2 2 time (two two time) than using the quaver or the eight note as a beat unit in the 6 8 time (six eight time) or the 2 4 time (two four time). Thirdly, different time signatures are by tradition associated with different styles of music. For example, because of how fast the music is, it might look rather odd to write a rock musical piece using the 4 8 time (four eight time) or the 4 2 time (four two time).

At the beginning of virtually any written piece of music you must have ever seen and will ever see, there are certain symbols and numbers just before the key signatures or the clef sign. These symbols and numbers help you understand how to interpret the musical notations on the musical piece in front of you. So far in our study, you've become familiar and been exposed to these symbols and by now you know that the numbers and symbols guide you on how to best interpret the rhythm of the music, and to keep track and keep count of the musical piece in time! Even better, when you play alongside several musical performers, the numbers and symbols help you stay together, so no one plays faster or slower than expected.

However, there are so many numbers and symbols and also so many ways for the numbers and symbols to be written in a musical piece, depending on the composer's choice.

Above are some of the likely time signature numbers and symbols you might have come across or will come across as you continue to play. Also in the above image, you'd notice that some time signatures are written in the form of letters instead of the regular numbers we are used to, which of course adds even more beauty and potential complications into the musical piece! These letters however really just substitute for the numbers with additional special meanings though, like I said, it all depends on the composer's choice.

From all these we have been discussing, the topic on time signatures raise certain questions like, " Why do we really need all these different time signatures for our music compositions?" "Do these time signatures really mean different things, or are they just there for fancy to make the grand staff look more beautiful?" "And why do different musical composers and performing musicians like better to use certain time signatures over others?"

Actually, all these time signatures with their different numbers and symbols really do have different meanings and different purposes in a given music piece, however, some of them can sound exactly the same to the human ear. Some of them are quite rare and not used very often while others are used as commonly as possible. Very shortly, I would answer all the aforementioned questions, that is, explain the fundamentals of reading time signatures (simple and compound) and meters, also show you how the different time signatures are related to one other and how they can sound both similar and different, and basically why different composers might decide to choose certain time signatures over others!

IMPORTANCE OF TIMING IN SOUND.

One of the fundamental elements in the definition of music itself is its movement through time, that is, music should move through time, music is not static like a signpost. Some scholars would define music as a pleasant sound that is organized through time. To help us in the composition of music through time as explained, managed and practiced in the Western music system, we use time signatures! That's how important they are, time signatures basically help us organize our musical pieces with the consideration of timing, hence the name, "Time signature".

The term "time signatures" clearly helps us to notate music (by giving time values to the beat required) with that, we would find it easy to play our music from the musical pieces, we can also listen to the composition patterns of the musical piece, and also discuss our music using more understandable terms when we discuss with our friends who are also music composers and performing musicians.

As notated by the time signatures, the compositional patterns of the beats in our music, is what and how we feel and hear the meter of the musical piece. When we discuss music with our friends who are performing musicians too, the terms time signature and meter are sometimes used in place of the other; however, time signature simply refers specifically to the different types and numbers of notes in each measure/bar of music while meter refers to the manner the notes are grouped together in the music measure most times in a repeated manner to create a very good musical composition pleasant to the ear. The different methods of classifying various time signatures into meters will be discussed later in this book.

METERS AND RHYTHMS

As discussed earlier, meter refers to the manner the notes are grouped together in the music measure most times in a repeated manner to create a very good musical composition pleasant to the ear. Some scholars would tell you that meter is the tool used to explain the movement of music through time, but composers and musicians have found another way that discusses the movement of music through time, they call it rhythm. Rhythms refers to the lengths of the notes in a given musical piece, rhythm is simply which notes are long and which notes are short and how they relate to each other in the music. With the help of time signatures, composers and musicians can play the rhythms of different musical pieces with ease.

In musical pieces and musical scores, music is organized and composed into measures or bars. A bar may also be referred to as a measure, a measure or a bar is the intersection of the five horizontal lines of the staff with another line vertically, this indicates a separation.

Every bar/measure has a particular number of notes that is allowed to be placed in it, and the number of notes in each measure is dependent on the time signature used in the musical piece.

The most commonly used notes that make up the short and long rhythms in the different meters are illustrated in the chart below, starting from the longest held notes and down to the shortest held notes. The chart also shows the relationship in length between the note values.

Symbol	Rhythm Name	Notation Name
	ta	Quarter Note
	ti-ti	2 Eighth Notes
	---	Quarter Note Rest
	tika-tika	4 Sixteenth Notes
	too	Half Note
	ti-tika	Eighth Note 2 Sixteenth Notes
	tika-ti	2 Sixteenth Notes Eighth Note
	tum-ti	Dotted Quarter Note Eighth Note
	syn-co-pa	Eighth Note, Quarter Note, Eighth Note
	tim-ka	Dotted Eighth Note Sixteenth Note

READING THE TIME SIGNATURES

As I said earlier, the particular number of notes permissible in every bar/measure is most times determined by the time signature used in the musical piece. As you have seen from several time signature examples, every time signature value has two numbers, a number on top and another number at the bottom, for instance, 2/4 time, 3/8 time, 9/8 time, 4/4 time, 2/2 time, 3/4 time, 6/8 time and so many other examples.

The number at the bottom of the time signature signifies a certain kind of note, usually the number of beats or note value that should be used, and the number at the top indicates how many of the notes should be in each bar/measure!

If you remember the American names of the note values (quarter, quaver, semi quaver...), there's a fun trick to it, let's play!

Let's take the 2 4(two four) time signature as our first example; with the number 2 at the top of the time signature, we know there should be 2 beats for one bar/measure, this then leaves us with a fraction of 1/4, and what is the name of the fraction 1/4? A quarter! Yes, a quarter! now we know that the time signature is indicating to us that the note length is a quarter note. Therefore, the 2/4 time means that there should be two quarter notes in every bar/measure, or two crotchet beats in every bar.

Let's try another example, In the 9/8 (nine eight) time signature, we know that in every bar/measure there should be 9 notes in a 1/8 length or nine quaver notes in every bar.

Let's try the 4/2 time, In the 4/2 time, we know that each measure should have 4 notes of 1/2, that is, four half notes in a every bar/measure or four minim beats in a bar/measure.

In the 3/1 time, we have 3 notes of a 1/1 notes, that is, three whole notes or three semibreve notes in every bar.

COMMON TIME AND CUT TIME

The above examples explain steps to help you figure out the numbers and notes of most time signatures, but when you have the two time signatures that are letters, what do you do? In fact, the time signatures that are letters are actually shorthand other styles for expressing the most common time signatures used by musicians.

The 4/4 (four four) time signature is so common that it has two forms and two names, the first is the 4/4 (four four), and the second is what we call "Common Time." So whenever you see "common time" in any musical piece, just know that it means the 4/4 time (four four time)

Another prevalent time signature is the 2/2 time (two two time). It is much like the Common Time signature, except that it has a slash through it. These measures (the 2/2 time) have four quarter notes in them too, but it is still called Cut Time, hence the slashed C or cut C." The Cut Time thus change to Common Time, this means that, it goes twice as fast as the original beat, instead of the quarter note or crotchet note getting the beat, the half note gets the beat!

CLASSIFICATION OF METERS

Explained above are the basic things you need to know about reading time signatures in any musical piece, and now we get to move to learning how the time signatures can best be understood as meters! In music, there are two levels for meter classification, the first level of meter classification is focused on the subdivision of the beat by the time signature.

In western music, there are only two ways to properly classify or subdivide beats into two or three smaller notes. The other subdivisons are either derived from the multiples of the two major subdivisions or from complex by adding them together. For easy notation and classification of the subdivisions as meters hence, we have; Simple Time, Compound Time, and Irregular Time.

SIMPLE TIME

A simple time is any meter in which the basic note are divided into groups of two. Among the examples of the simple time meters include the time signatures such as the common Time, cut Time, 4/4 time (four four time), 2/4 time (two four time), 2/2 time (two two time). These meters are referred to as simple time signatures because the quarter note can be equally divided into two eighth notes, or the half-note can equally divide into two other quarter notes, or the whole note can equally divide into two separate half notes.

COMPOUND TIME

The compound time is a little bit more complicated than the simple time. The compound time is any meter with basic notes divisible into groups of three. To help you easily identify a compound time, whenever you see an 8 as the number at the bottom of the time signature value, you know it's not a simple time but a compound time.

Using an 8 to mean a simple time would not make sense. So, whenever you look through a musical piece and you find an 8 as the number at the bottom of your time signature, you should know, from our explanation that your eighth notes/ quaver notes should be together in groups of three and not two.

In 6/8 time (six eight time) for example, there are two groups of three eighth-notes or group of three quaver notes. In the 9/8 time (nine eight time) there are three groups of three eighth notes or three quaver notes. In the 12/8 time (twelve eight time) there are four groups of three eighth notes or four groups of three quaver notes.

IRREGULAR TIME

The last example of beat subdivisions is the unequal or irregular subdivision of the beat, in this subdivision, every other time signature value that is not simple or compound time is covered! Even though they are called irregular meters, they also have patterns which can be understood by a professional piano player. The most common examples of irregular meters only combine compound time and simple time in one single measure. Making each measure have beats with three subdivisions and also beats with two subdivisions.

Examples of the irregular time include the time signatures 5/8 time (five eight time) and 7/8 time (seven eight time). But because there are 5 eighth notes per bar/measure in the 5/8 time or 7 eighth notes per bar/measure in the 7/8 time, it is difficult to have equal groups of two or three eighth notes. So what do we do? Just like in the 6/8 time (six eight time), 9/8time (nine eight time), and the 12/8 time (twelve eight time), where the groups of eighth-notes are joined together by a beam to make a larger count, the same is done in the 5/8 time (five eight time) and the 7/8 time(seven eight time), they are joined together by a beam to make a larger count too. But in the 5/8 time (five eight time) and the 7/8 time (seven eight time) because the number on top in the time signature is an odd and prime number, the length of each bar/measure is irregular or uneven. The eighth note at the bottom stays at the same length, but just because some of the counts have two eight notes and other counts have three eighth notes, they are referred to as irregular!

DUPLE, TRIPLE, AND QUADRUPLE

The second degree for classifying meters is determining how many beats that are present in a measure. There are three types in this classification, and the most common types are the duple (2/2 time, 2/4 time and the 6/8 time) then we have the triple (3/4 time, 9/8 time and the 3/2 time), and the quadruple (4/4 time, 12/8 time and the 4/2 time). A duple has two beats in a bar/measure, a triple has three beats in a bar/measure, and a quadruple has four beats in a bar/measure.

The Cut-Time or the 2/2 time (two two time) is a duple meter and a simple meter because there are only two beats in the bar/measure and the beats can be divided by two.

The 3/4 time (three four time) is a triple meter and a simple meter because there are only three beats in the bar/measure and the beats can be divided by two.

The 4/2 time (four two time) is a quadruple meter and a simple meter because there are only four beats in the bar measure and the beats can be divided by two.

The 6/8 time (six eight time) is a duple and a compound meter because there are only two beats in the bar/measure and the beats can be divided by three.

The 9/8 time (nine eight time) is a triple and a compound meter because there are only three beats in the bar/measure and the beats can be divided by three.

The 5/8 time (five eight time) is a duple and an irregular meter because there are only two beats in the bar/measure and the beats can be divided irregularly.

From the above explanations, we can see that there are certain similarities and slight differences between all the time signatures and their meters. For instance, all the quadruple and duple time meters are the same in that they have two and four beats in each bar/measure. This characteristics makes the sounds produced by the two measures sound the same to the human ear. Simple and triple time meter music pieces can sound like compound pieces depending on the tempo of the music piece. While some other compound pieces like the 6/8 time (six eight time) can sound like a simple beat subdivision. For instance, a 6/8 time (six eight time) sounding like a 3/4 time (three four time). However, what helps us to easily differentiate a lot of these meters is their beat hierarchies and the different styles of music they are used in.

HIERARCHY OF BEATS

As we already know, music is sound composed through time and what the time signature helps us do is, tell us how best to structure and organize music in time. One very important aspect within the time signature, is knowing which beats and which notes that are more important and as such should be accented. This beat accentuation is otherwise known as beat hierarchy.

 In virtually all classic western music, the first beat in every bar/measure is usually considered the strongest and the most important beat in that bar/measure, thus, it carries the most weight in the composition. However, in duple meters, the second beat is usually weak and any of the subdivisions of the said beat is usually weaker. The third beat in the measure of a quadruple meter is usually stronger than the second beat, but it is not as strong as the first beat, and the fourth beat usually leads into the first beat of the next measure called a downbeat. In triple time, the meter starts with a strong first beat, then a weak second beat, and then it begins to build on the third beat, which then leads back to the first beat.

Understanding the hierarchies of beats in different time signatures should help you play any musical score or musical piece, especially with those that use very little articulation, knowing the strongest and weakest beats to play will help a great deal.

CHAPTER FOUR:

Musical Scales

A scale is any given group of pitches or scale degrees that are arranged in ascending order. The pitches create an octave. Diatonic scales are those scales that have whole and half steps included. The first and the last note of a scale is called the tonic. It is the easiest note to find and it's also the most stable note. . The other notes that make up the scale also have their own uunique names. The second note of the scale is also known as the Supertonic. The third note is known as the mediant, that is, the note that is halfway between the tonic note and the dominant note. The fourth note of the scale is known as the subdominant. The fifth note of the scale is called the Dominant. The sixth note is called the submediant. IN the natural minor scale, the seventh note is referred to as the subtonic note, while in the major, melodic and harmonic minor scales, the seventh note is known as the leading note. (it is one half step lower that the last note, known as the tonic)

THE MAJOR SCALE

The major scale is made up of seven different pitches or scale degrees. In the major scale, there are half steps between the third and the fourth and the seventh and the eighth scale degrees; While there are whole steps between all the other degrees. Below is how the C major scale looks like. The way the pattern of the whole and half steps here is the same for all the major scales. Just by altering the first note and using this pattern as a guide, you can create any major scale.

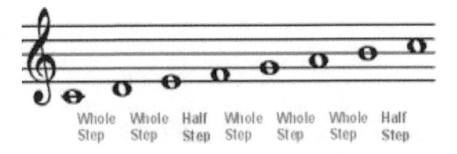

THE NATURAL MINOR SCALE

The natural minor scale have seven different pitches or scale degrees. The natural minor scales have half steps between the second and the third degree and the fifth and sixth degrees; there are whole steps between all the other steps.

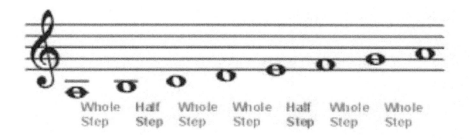

THE HARMONIC MINOR SCALE

The harmonic minor scale is the same as the natural minor scale, only that the seventh degree is raised by half a step. That creates an interval of a half step between the seventh and eighth degrees, and an interval of one and a half steps between the sixth and the seventh notes.

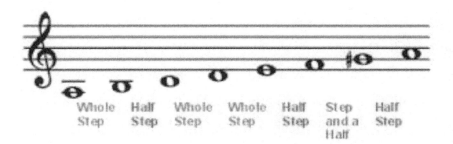

THE MELODIC MINOR SCALE

The melodic minor is another type of minor scale. Here, the sixth and the seventh notes are both raised by one half step.

139

PENTATONIC SCALES

Pentatonic scales have only five notes. The gaps from one end of the scale to the other are all more than half a step.

THE RELATIVE MINOR SCALE

A relative minor scale is usually used in music improvisation, because it gives more ideas to a musical piece or a solo. All what the piano player or the improviser needs to do is learn about the major and minor scales and also learn how to use the relative minor scale. What then is the relative minor scale?

Let's take the C major scale as our first example. The relative minor scale of the C major scale will be A minor. Why? Here's a simple rule to guide you when determining the relative minor of any major scale. The relative minor scale of a major scale is the minor scale of the sixth note of its tonality. This may sound confusing but this is what I mean, the relative minor of any major scale is the sixth note of the major scale. As we see in C major, the sixth note is A, so to get the minor scale of C major, just play the A minor scale.

RELATIONSHIP BETWEEEN THE MAJOR SCALE AND THE RELATIVE MINOR SCALE

When we compare the C major scale and the A minor scale, we see that they have exactly the same notes. Meaning that the major scale always has a related minor that is identical to it. Amazing, isn't it? This is why the word "relative" is used.

Let's look at some examples, starting with the C major scale and its relative minor scale, A minor;

The C major scale: C , D , E , F , G , A , B

The A minor scale: A , B , C , D , E , F , G

Another example is the G major major scale and its relative minor, the E minor scale.

The G major scale: G , A , B , C , D , E , F #

The E minor scale: E , F # , G , A , B , C

How interesting this is, It means that we can use the A minor scale to do an improvisation or a solo in a song originally written in the C major scale. In other words, when we have a major scale, we can go ahead and think of two scales: the major scale and its relative minor scale. This increases our options when we play, so what we play and what people hear are all in one word, INTERESTING!

We could also think I the opposite direction: each minor scale has a relative major scale. This relative major is a tone and a half above the minor scale. For instance, one tone and a half above A is C! interesting yea? You can try the same trick for other minor scales too.

The C Major Scale

The C major is a major scale based on the music alphabet C, with the different pitches as C, D , E , F , G , A , and B. C major is perhaps one of the most common key signatures used today. Its key signature has zero flats and sharps. Its relative minor scale is the A minor scale and its parallel minor scale is the C minor scale.

Let's take a look at the C major scale in history, how and where it was used by famous composers in their compositions.

20 out of Joseph Hadyn's 104 symphonies were composed using the C major scale, making it his second most used scale, his first was D major. 33 out of the 134 symphonies mistakenly attributed to Joseph Hadyn by H.C Robbins were written in C major, more than any other key.

In the classical era, many settings and masses of Te deum were in C major. Many of W.A Mozart's masses were in C major, same with Joseph Hadyn.

Franz Schubert's two symphonies in the C major key. The first one was nicknamed the "Little C major" while the second was nicknamed the "Great C major".

"The Entertainer" by Scott Joplin was written in the C major key.

Many musicians both in the past and contemporary have made us understand that every single musical key produces a unique feeling. Popular American songwriter Bob Dylan once mentioned that the C major key is the key of strength.

CHAPTER FIVE:

Piano Hand Coordination

No piano lesson is complete without the knowledge of the three Cs, what are the three Cs? They are; Concentration, coordination and confidence. And they three together have their different meanings but are sure to guide you on a successful practice routine from being an amateur to being a professional piano player. Of the three, coordination is presumed to be the trickiest, it is often regarded as the hardest to fully grasp, but of course you know that it is not more important as the other two, they work together as a unit.

In learning any instrument at all, whether the guitar, the drums or the saxophone, in this case the piano, the understanding of how the three Cs work is very important, particularly Coordination, because as we know, the piano is one of the instruments we play with both our hands involved in the action. Coordination therefore, ensures that you play with both hands comfortably to a point where you do not make mistakes anymore. Worthy of mention is the fact that the piano in fact requires the use of both hands for the keys and also the feet for the dampers! Now you see the importance of coordination to help you use both hands and your feet simultaneously as you play.

The problem of coordination is unsurprisingly a problem for most beginner players, especially those who are very used to using one hand. The problem takes a notch higher when the beginner watches a professional piano player use both hands and feet perfectly while performing a musical score. It's the same as rubbing your stomach and tapping your head both at the same time, tricky yea?

Despite the seeming difficulty in mastering the hand coordination, musicians and piano players know the importance of learning hand coordination at the preliminary stages of playing the piano, it is a very essential skill to learn! It's the same with other instruments too like the guitar, drums, organ etc. these instruments have a lot to do with developing a very good hand coordination as well as strong muscle memory. This is not to scare you but to prepare your mind to learn the skill! Yes! The skill of hand coordination can be learned, because it's really not something any musician is born with, they learnt it too at a point in their training. Hence, the importance of consistent practice! Practice actually improves and develops hand coordination.

Below are outlined some tips that would help you develop a good hand coordination, although the tips are not hard and fast rules, they are simply guides to set you on your journey in mastering the skill.

1. One hand at a Time

In the process of learning a new piece, it's rather advisable and a very good idea to learn with your left hand (or whichever hand is your weaker hand) part first before you try with your stronger hand. As a beginner new to playing any musical instrument or the piano for instance, you'd discover that the weaker hand would actually need more time to play its part than the stronger hand. So, take it one hand at a time!

2. Practice Counterpoint

When playing the piano, organ, drums, guitar or any instrument that requires the use of your hands, you should learn how to play different rhythms using both hands. Meaning, you should learn how to coordinate both hands to play different rhythms. One way you can learn that fast is by using the left hand to tap out the quarter notes or the crotchet notes (you remember the quarter notes yea?) and using the right hand to play out the eight notes or the quaver notes and vice versa. This is called counterpoint in keyboard practice, it involves the use of both hands to play different melodies. As this is a good way to develop a good hand coordination, it is however, a more advanced exercise.

3. Play Quiet

Yes! Piano hand coordination exercises can be practiced silently. You can easily perform the exercises using your tables. This is a regular practice style for drummers though, who sometimes their drum sticks over pillows or tables. Exercises of this manner actually help to develop the memory of the hand muscles. You can perform the exercises without planning for them, you can do them while you watch TV or while you perform other tasks.

4. Exercise your hands

By strengthening your hand muscles physically is one sure way to improve your hand coordination. How? Just the same way some guitar players exercise their playing hand by squeezing tennis balls to build the muscles, you can use one of those or some other finger strengtheners like Fingerweights or even stress balls can do too.

5. Back and forth

This is perhaps one of the most efficient hand coordination exercises. Place both hands on the keyboard as if you're ready to play. Make sure both your left and right thumbs are resting on the middle C, and the other four fingers on the four white keys away from the middle C. Now play the scale with your right hand first and then with the left hand. Now play the same thing but this time starting with your left pinky finger all the way up to right pinky finger and then back again!

6. Warm up

Practicing scales and other rudiments are very essential to improving your hand coordination. These scales should be played at the start of every piano practice, see them more as warm up exercises to get you ready to go. So you do not get bored on the way, you can learn different scales to have a lot of options to always choose from and always switch between your choices.

7. Take it slow

Whether or not you learn your hand coordination by practicing scales or other rudiments, here's a trick that should work for you, when you start to practice the scales, take it slow at first, with this your hands are slowly grasping the correct technique, also learning to play very clean and also learning to avoid bad habits as you go. Although, it's okay to watch out for your weaker hand by looking at t as you play, but when you are sure you have the right technique, you can continue with the exercise without looking at the hand, and also at a faster pace this time.

8. Use a metronome

Drummers use a metronome while playing to maintain steady strokes when practicing their rudiments. Metronomes are very god tools used during hand coordination exercises. It is advisable to musicians especially piano players to use a metronome while practicing scales and other rudiments.

9. Slow and steady

Another very helpful technique when practicing hand coordination is
to press the keys very slowly without looking at your fingers. This will
increase your conversance with the keys using your fingers. This is
done by placing your fingers on the keyboard in play position and
slowly playing the scales making yourself conversant with each key as
you play, how they feel and sound when each key is pressed.

10. The other way round

This tip is helpful for the keyboard hand coordination and for other
instruments too. When you start to learn a new piece on the
keyboard, play the melody for the right hand with the left hand. By
doing this, you will increase the creativity and mobility of your left
hand.

Fingering

Fingerings are all about which of your fingers you are meant to use and also the apparent position of your hand while you play the piano. However, there are guiding rules for fingerings and finger positions used generally depending on the type of music and the situation of the musical performance.

While you exercise using scales, it is very important to use the correct fingerings, it's like using the right tool for the right job! By doing this, you build yourself on a very strong foundation of development of a good playing technique. On some piano sheet music, you will find instructions telling you what fingers to use during playing, most if not all of those piano sheets use the number 1 - 5

1 is the thumb, the big thumb

2 is the index finger, the finger just after the thumb

3 is the middle finger, next to the index finger

4 is the ring finger, in between the middle finger and the little finger

5 is the little finger or pinky.

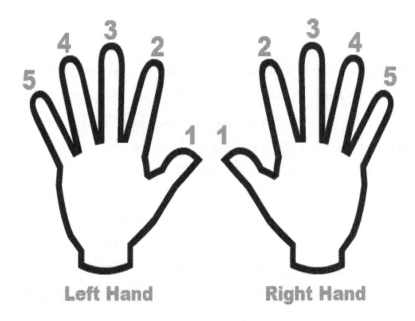

Some tips on how to position your hand and fingers while you play.

The way and manner your hands move and the fingers you use while playing greatly affects the results of your piano practice and playing. For example, if you use fewer fingers for high frequencies, your transitions will be irregular when they should be smooth. To help you, here are some outlined guidelines:

- First on the list is this, do not at any time exclusively use your index finger. Meaning do not always use your first finger anytime you play, most beginners actually pick up that habit when they start to play.

- When playing, use all your fingers, this will help the movement of your hand to be smoother.

- Also, very important too, avoid using your thumb to play the black keys.

- Try playing the piano without looking down at it, this will help your confidence and also improve your hand coordination and muscle memory.

Most piano players and musicians who study how the piano works will overtime know how to read the notes on piano sheets. There is nothing difficult actually in knowing or learning how to read from the piano sheets, but the real issue is reading and playing at the same time. But the good news is, with more and more practice on hand coordination, regardless of the number of notes you have on the sheet, the fewer the times you would look down at the piano.

However, this requires much practice before it can be achieved but what's noteworthy is to know how well to position your fingers, how well to use your hands correctly and how well to master a good fingering technique. When using all of your fingers, you do not have to change your hand position or use the same finger to play multiple keys, this is something to note especially when you're playing with very few glances at the keyboard.

The first finger sequence is 1 – 2 – 3 – 1 – 2 – 3 – 4 - 5, and this sequence involves the movement of the thumb under the middle and index fingers. After you complete the next octave, turn around again but this time the other way round by moving your index and middle fingers over your thumb 5 – 4 – 3 – 2 – 1 – 3 – 2 – 1 .

The secret is simple, all you need to do is to move your thumb under the index and middle fingers and lift those same fingers over your thumb. Using this method, you can complete eight notes/one octave on the piano keyboard by slight movements of the hands.

Don't worry, this may look confusing at first but with time you'd get a hang of it. Also, the above fingering pattern 1-2-3-1-2-3-4-5 does not apply to all situations. The Major C scale for example is best suited to use the fingering pattern. In some other situations that may involve another scale, a different fingering pattern could be more appropriate. However, the most important thing to do is to play as natural as possible and try to involve all your fingers.

In the cases where the fingering patterns are not written out, it should not be a problem for you. All you need to do is try to avoid using your thumb on the black keys and you will naturally find yourself practicing with the right fingering technique.

Piano fingering simply refers to the placement of the fingers on the keyboard of the piano and it could also mean the hand techniques used when playing the piano. In every fingered piano musical sheet, the sheet marks every note with a finger number that matches one of the five fingers indicating the right finger to use to play the note.

The fingered piano sheet is designed to help a beginner pianist know the right finger to be used to play each note, however, it also helps even the most skilled piano players in knowing the most appropriate technique to play a musical piece. Different musical notes may have finger patterns in sheet music, but chords do not usually have fingered marks. However, there are fingering patterns and hand formations that could be used when playing chords.

Reading Fingered Piano Music

In fingered piano music, you will find numbers 1 to 5 scribbled above or below the notes of songs and scales. The numbers actually match the five human fingers telling us which finger should play which key. . The numbering of the finger is expressed as follows:

Thumb: 1

Index Finger: 2

Middle Finger: 3

Ring Finger: 4

Pinky Finger: 5

Fingered Practice Scales

A good fingering technique is a very valuable skill you should have as a pianist. When you do practice fingering techniques, you train your fingers to develop new playing techniques, and also get used to hand positions, and also help you exercise flexibility and speed. The actual practice of fingering may look difficult at first trial, but just keep practicing until your fingers get used to it.

For a start, there exists a number of hand technique exercises that can help you develop and strengthen your piano fingering skill. You can begin by ascending scales and then continue with descending scales. On some piano sheets, you will find a mark like a slur, it only tells you that is where the thumb should cross under the other fingers(the index and middle fingers) in order to play the next note of the scale.

For instance, if the first five notes of a regular scale is labeled as 1, 2, 3, 4, 1. Between 4 and 1, on the piano fingering sheet, you would find a slur telling you to move the under the middle and index fingers to play the fifth note.

Also, you can practice different fingering techniques by playing pentatonic scales or five-note scales. You can do this by playing the first five notes of the different scales, starting with the C scale, then the D scale, E scale and so on.

Piano Chord Fingering

The fingering for a piano chord is sometimes the same with both your left and right hands, it is only reversed. To help you play the chords in some piano sheets without fingering, here are a few guides;

Triad chords or three notes in the root position are mostly formed using the fingers 1 – 3 - 5 (that is, the thumb finger, the middle finger and the pinky finger). For instance, in a C chord using the right hand, it would be played with the first finger, the thumb on C, the third finger or the middle finger on E and the fifth finger or the pinky on G.

Some piano players often form four notes or tetrad chords using the fingers 1 – 2 – 3 - 5 (the thumb, the index finger, the middle finger and the pinky) also the fingering using the fingers 1 - 2 - 4 - 5 (the thumb, the index finger, the ring finger and the pinky) can be used too.

Ideally, the flexibility and size of your fingers will go a long way to determine the position of your fingers for larger chords.

Some fingering rules.

The piano fingering pattern always alternates between 1 2 3 1 2 3 4 or 3 2 1 4 3 2 1, this happens so that the exact same pattern is repeated with every octave.

Never play your thumb on the black keys, only on the white keys.

Play your ring finger or fourth finger on a black key when there is a black key among the keys of the scale .

Always play your pinky or fifth finger at a starting point, a stopping point, or a turning-around point, so your finger movement is not disjointed.

When playing out scales in music, you can try fingering techniques that help the fingering patterns of both hands align. For instance, you can try to make both your thumbs play together at a point in the scale.

THE FINGERING CHART

RIGHT-HANDED SCALE FINGERINGS FOR MAJOR KEYS

MAJOR KEY (s)	FINGERING
C Major Scale	1-2-3-1-2-3-4-5
F Major Scale	1-2-3-4-1-2-3-4
B♭ Major Scale	2-1-2-3-1-2-3-4
E♭ Major Scale	2-1-2-3-4-1-2-3
A♭ Major Scale	2-3-1-2-3-1-2-3
D♭ Major Scale	2-3-1-2-3-4-1-2
G♭ or F# Major Scale	2-3-4-1-2-3-1-2
B Major Scale	1-2-3-1-2-3-4-5
E Major Scale	1-2-3-1-2-3-4-5
A Major Scale	1-2-3-1-2-3-4-5
D Major Scale	1-2-3-1-2-3-4-5
G Major Scale	1-2-3-1-2-3-4-5

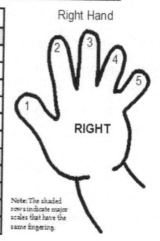

Right Hand

RIGHT

Note: The shaded rows indicate major scales that have the same fingering.

LEFT-HANDED SCALE FINGERINGS FOR MAJOR KEYS

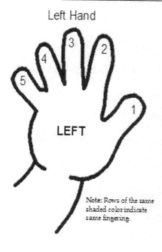

Left Hand

LEFT

Note: Rows of the same shaded color indicate same fingering.

MAJOR KEY (s)	FINGERING
C Major Scale	5-4-3-2-1-3-2-1
F Major Scale	5-4-3-2-1-3-2-1
B♭ Major Scale	3-2-1-4-3-2-1-3
E♭ Major Scale	3-2-1-4-3-2-1-3
A♭ Major Scale	3-2-1-4-3-2-1-3
D♭ Major Scale	3-2-1-4-3-2-1-3
G♭ or F# Major Scale	4-3-2-1-3-2-1-2
B Major Scale	4-3-2-1-4-3-2-1
E Major Scale	5-4-3-2-1-3-2-1
A Major Scale	5-4-3-2-1-3-2-1
D Major Scale	5-4-3-2-1-3-2-1
G Major Scale	5-4-3-2-1-3-2-1

The fingering chart provides the best piano keyboard scale fingering patterns. It is however not the traditional fingering pattern for scale that is commonly taught.

The piano as an instrument is somewhat has the capacity to produce a beautiful variety of functions in music. Music lovers especially, piano players and music composers use the piano to perform several functions, from creating great musical symphonies and pieces, to writing harmonies and melodies for songs and choruses.

The piano keyboard is so powerful that it is believed as a link between practical music and music theory. It is rather mandatory for every music performer and composer or all musicians generally to be familiar with the keyboard, doing that also learning a few fingering exercises and hand technique to help them become better.

Shortly we will examine some exercises to help you strengthen and build your finger strength, muscle memory and hand flexibility. To enjoy the best benefits from these exercises and get the best out of it, I suggest you use a keyboard if you do not have access to a piano.

For the exercises, I will show you how the music theory relates to how you use your fingers to play the piano keyboard. That is why I earlier mentioned that every music performer and composer should in a way be familiar with the keyboard because it is a pointer to what music theory is about. The keys of the piano are already perfect illustrations of scales, intervals and notes in music, and can help you in understanding any pitched instrument. A very effective piano fingering exercise helps you develop not only flexibility, but a great understanding of how music works generally.

As a way of introduction, we will begin the piano fingering exercises with the major and minor scales. The musical scales are the step-by-step sequence of notes found in music keys. By learning basic scales, you teach your hands to play differently, and when you fully perfect it, it will help you understand the basic chords and how to play them.

All the scales both the major and minor scales are built on easy formulae that have not changed and never will. These formulae are nothing but a series of whole steps, half steps and intervals on the keyboard. To help you build major keys, here is a formula you might need to memorize. Starting with the C major scale;

WN – WN – HN – WN – WN – WN - HN

C D E F G A B C

Starting with the C note, if you follow closely, by looking at the formula, you will get the exact notes in the scale above. You can try building the major scales of different keys using the formula.

Using the same formula, we can also build minor scales too; for instance, the A minor scale;

WN - HN - WN - WN - HN - WN - WN

A B C D E F G A

WN – Whole note

HN – Half note

Now that we have learnt how to build the major and minor scales, let's learn the fingers to use;

FINGERING PATTERNS FOR C, D, E, G AND A MAJOR AND MINOR SCALES

If you remember what we discussed on the Circle of 5ths, the keys (C, D, E, G and A) are actually the first five keys on the side of the chart with sharps. Moving from C to G to D to A and then finally to E, we will be adding one sharp to the scale of every major scale we play.

The fingering pattern for the scales are similar, making them very good piano fingering exercises. Below are the fingering patterns you should know for both hands.

Fingerings for the left hand: 5 – 4 – 3 – 2 – 1 – 3 – 2 - 1

Fingerings for the right hand: 1 - 2 - 3 - 1 - 2 - 3 - 4 - 5

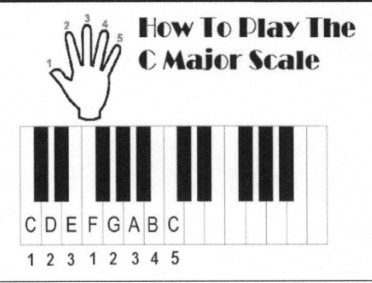

Now using the fingering pattern above, you can try to practice these scales below, try out slowly first;

C Major:

 The Notes: C – D – E – F – G – A – B - C

C Minor:

The Notes: C - D – E b - F - G – A b – B b - C

G Major:

The Notes: G – A – B – C – D – E – F # - G

G Minor:

The Notes: G - A – B b - C - D – E b - F- G

D Major:

The Notes: D – E – F # - G – A – B – C # - D

D Minor:

The Notes: D - E - F - G - A – B b - C - D

A Major:

The Notes: A – B – C # - D – E – F # - G # - A

A Minor:

The Notes: A - B - C - D - E - F - G - A

E Major:

The Notes: E – F # - G # - A – B – C # - D # - E

E Minor:

The Notes: E – F # - G - A - B - C - D - E

The third finger or middle finger for both hands should line up at all times, just in case they don't, you can stop and try again. Like I said earlier, you can start really slow that increase tempo when you feel more confident in yourself. Also, as soon as possible, start to practice with a metronome. A metronome will help you develop your rhythm internally as you play.

LEARNING OTHER SCALES

After you must have mastered the fingering patterns for major and minor scales in C, G, D, A, and E like we have done, now you are ready to practice tougher scales.

As you can see below, the scales do not have similar fingering pattern like we had in the previous exercise. Here too, the middle fingers of both hands do not play together

B Major:

The Notes: B – C # - D # - E – F # - G # - A # - B

Fingering for the left hand: 4 – 3 – 2 – 1 – 4 – 3 – 2 - 1

Fingerings for the right hand: 1 - 2 - 3 - 1 - 2 - 3 - 4 - 5

C # / D b Major:

The Notes: D b – E b - F – G b – A b – B b - C – D b

Fingerings for the left hand: 3 - 2 - 1 - 4 - 3 - 2 – 1 - 3

Fingerings for the right hand: 2 – 3 – 1 – 2 – 3 – 4 – 1 - 2

D # / E b Major:

The Notes: E b - F - G – A b – B b - C - D – E b

Fingerings for the left hand: 3 - 2 - 1 - 4 - 3 - 2 - 1 - 3

Fingerings for the right hand: 3 - 1 – 2 – 3 – 4 – 1 – 2 - 3

F # / G b Major:

The Notes: F # - G # - A # - B – C # - D # - F – F #

Fingerings for the left hand: 4 - 3 - 2 - 1 - 3 - 2 - 1 - 4

Fingerings for the right hand: 2 – 3 – 4 – 1 – 2 – 3 – 1 - 2

G #/ A b Major:

The Notes: A b – B b - C – D b – E b - F - G – A b

Fingerings for the left hand: 3 - 2 - 1 - 4 - 3 - 2 - 1 - 3

Fingerings for the right hand: 3 – 4 – 1 – 2 – 3 – 1 – 2 - 3

A # / B b Major:

The Notes: B b - C - D – E b - F - G - A – B b

Fingerings for the left hand: 3 - 2 - 1 - 4 - 3 - 2 - 1 - 3

Fingerings for the right hand: 4 – 1 – 2 – 3 – 1 – 2 – 3 - 4

A # / B b Minor:

The Notes: A # - C – C # - D # - F – F # - G # - A #

Fingerings for the left hand: 2 - 1 - 3 - 2 - 1 - 4 - 3 - 2

Fingerings for the right hand: 2 – 1 – 2 – 3 – 1 – 2 – 3 - 4

B Minor:

The Notes: B – C # - D - E – F # - G - A - B

Fingerings for the left hand: 4 - 3 - 2 - 1 - 4 - 3 - 2 - 1

Fingerings the right hand: 1 – 2 – 3 – 1 – 2 – 3 – 4 - 5

C # / D b Minor:

The Notes: C # - D # - E – F # - G # - A - B – C #

Fingerings for the left hand: 3 - 2 - 1 - 4 - 3 - 2 - 1 - 3

Fingerings for the right hand: 3 – 4 – 1 – 2 – 3 – 1 – 2 - 3

D #/E b Minor:

The Notes: D # - F – F # - G # - A # - B – C # - D #

Fingerings for the left hand: 2 - 1- 4- 3- 2- 1- 3- 2

Fingerings for the right hand: 3 - 1 - 2 - 3 - 4 - 1 - 2 - 3

F Minor:

The Notes: F - G – A b – B b - C - D b – E b - F

Fingerings for the left hand: 5 - 4 -3 – 2 – 1 – 3 – 2 - 1

Fingerings for the right hand: 1 - 2 - 3 - 4 - 1 - 2 - 3 – 4

F # / G b Minor:

The Notes: F # - G # - A - B – C # - D - E – F #

Fingerings for the left hand: 4 - 3 - 2 - 1 - 3 - 2 – 1 - 4

Fingerings for the right hand: 2 - 3 - 1 - 2 - 3 - 1 - 2 - 3

G # / A b Minor:

The Notes: G # - A # - B – C # - D # - E – F # - G #

Fingerings for the left hand: 3 -2 - 1 - 3 - 2 - 1 - 3 - 2

Fingerings for the right hand: 3 - 4 - 1 - 2 - 3 - 1 – 2 - 3

Below are some fingering exercises you can practice on the keyboard! Have fun!

INCY WINCY SPI-DER

C C C D E E

① ① ① ② ③ ③

CLIMBED UP THE WAT-ER SPOUT

E   D C D   E C

③   ② ① ②   ③ ①

DOWN CAME THE RAIN,

E   E   F   G

③   ③   ④   ⑤

AND WASHED THE SPI-DER OUT

G   F   E   F   G   E

⑤   ④   ③   ④   ⑤   ③

OUT CAME THE SUN AND

C   C   D   E   E

①   ①   ②   ③   ③

DRIED UP ALL THE RAIN, AND

D   C D   E   C   C

②   ① ②   ③   ①   ①

INCY WINCY SPI-DER

C C C D E E

① ① ① ② ③ ③

CLIMBED UP THE SPOUT A-GAIN

E   D C D   E C

③   ② ① ②   ③ ①

171

TWINKLE TWINKLE LITTLE STAR
C   C   G   G   A   A   G
①   ①   ⑤   ⑤ [STEP] ⑤   ⑤ [STEP] ⑤

HOW I   WONDER WHAT YOU ARE,
F   F   E   E   D   D   C
④   ④   ③   ③   ②   ②   ①

UP ABOVE THE WORLD SO HIGH
G   G   F   F   E   E   D
⑤   ⑤   ④   ④   ③   ③   ②

LIKE A DIAMOND IN THE SKY
G   G   F   F   E   E   D
⑤   ⑤   ④   ④   ③   ③   ②

TWINKLE TWINKLE LITTLE STAR
C   C   G   G   A   A   G
①   ①   ⑤   ⑤ [STEP] ⑤   ⑤ [STEP] ⑤

HOW I   WONDER WHAT YOU ARE,
F   F   E   E   D   D   C
④   ④   ③   ③   ②   ②   ①

MA-RY HAD A LIT-TLE LAMB

E D C D E E E

③ ② ① ② ③ ③ ③

LIT-TLE LAMB, LIT-TLE LAMB

D D D E E E

② ② ② ③ ③ ③

MA-RY HAD A LIT-TLE LAMB

E D C D E E E

③ ② ① ② ③ ③ ③

ITS FLEECE WAS WHITE AS SNOW

E D D E D C

③ ② ② ③ ② ①

CHAPTER SIX:

History Of The Solfa System

The solfa is a form of music education style that is used to teach aural musical skills as well as sight-reading in Western music.

In the solfa system, certain syllables are designated to musical notes of the scale to help the music performer audiate or hear mentally the piece of music he or she is seeing for the first tme to help them sing aloud. During the the Renaissance era, there were several 4, 5 and 6-note systems that were used to cover the entire octave. The tonic sol-fa system then somehow made the seven commonly used syllables popular, these syllables were mostly used in countries whose official language was English. The syllables include: do, re, mi, fa, so, la, and si or ti.

Currently, there are two ways of applying the solfa system or the solfege, 1. The fixed 'doh', here, the different syllables are attached to certain pitches, for example, "doh" is always attached to C natural.

2. The movable doh, here the different syllables are attached to scale degrees, for example, "doh" is always the first in the major scale).

Etymology of the Solfege or the solfa system.

The Italian "solfeggio" and the English or French "solfège" are both derived from the name of two of the syllables used in the system; sol and fa.

The generic menaiing of the word solfege is "solmization" and it refers to any system that involves assigning syllables to different pitches in the musical scale. The French meaning of the word solfege "solmisatio" is derived from the Latin solfège syllables sol and mi.

And the verb "to sol-fa" actually means to sing a piece in the solfège

Origin of the solfege

In Italy during the Eleventh century, a music theorist known as Guido of Arezzo invented a system of music notation that gave names to the the six note after the first syllable in each line of the Latin hymn Ut queant laxis, a "Hymn to St. John the Baptist".

In 1600, "Ut" was changed to the syllable "doh" in Italy, this was suggested by the musicologue, Giovanni Battista Doni, because of the first syllable of his surname "Doni". And Si was derived from the initials of "Sancte Iohannes", and was later added to complete the diatonic scale. In English speaking countries, "si" was later changed to "ti" in the Nineteenth century by Sarah Glover, according to her so that every one of the syllables should begin with a different letter.

In the Elizabethan Era

During the Elizabethan era in England, England and its surrounding territories used just four of the syllables; mi, fa, sol, and la. "Mi" represented the modern si, while "fa" the modern doh or ut, "sol" stood for the modern re, and "la" for the modern mi. Then, fa, sol and la were repeated to stand in for their modern alterations, making the scale look like; "fa, sol, la, fa, sol, la, mi, fa".

The solfege in modern times.

The Solfège is still being used for training in sight-reading. In the United States, the first traditional American country music was recorded around the 1920s by singers trained in the solfege, who were too poor to afford a piano but used sight reading to develop printed music for their own entertainment.

The solfege has two main types:

The Movable doh and the Fixed doh.

Movable doh solfège

In the Movable doh solfege, or what we call the tonic sol-fa, each syllable corresponds to a degree in the scale, and it is mostly used in Commonwealth Countries, Germanic countriesand the United States of America

The advantage of the movable doh solfege is in its ability to guide musicians in the understanding of music theory; because I the movable doh solfege, a tonic is established and then sung for comparison. Hence, the fixed doh is more appealing to instrumentalists, while the movable doh is applicable to music theorists and music composers.

The movable doh is frequently used in countries like Australia, Japan, Ireland, The United Kingdom, the United States, Canada and Hong Kong. In the movable doh solfege, each syllable of the solfege corresponds degree in the scale and to a pitch: The first degree in a major scale is usually sung as "doh", and the second "re", etc.

The syllables of the solfege used in the movable doh are slighty different from those used in the fixed doh solfege, this is because the English difference in the syllables "ti" instead of "si" is always used, as well as other altered syllables.

Musical pieces written in a minor key may be sol-faed in one of the two ways used in movable doh: either you start on doh using "me", "le", and "te" as the lowered third, sixth, and seventh notes, and "la" and "ti" as the raised sixth and seventh notes, this is referred to as doh-based minor, or you can start on la using "fi" and "si" as the raised sixth and seventh notes.

Fixed Doh.

In the Fixed doh, each of the syllables correspond to the name of a particular note. This is the same thing as done in the Romance system of naming different pitches according to the syllables of the solfege, and it is still being used in Slavic and Romance countries, including countries with official language as Spanish.

In the major Slavic and Romance language, the syllables Do, Re, mi, Fa, Sol, La, and Si are employed to name the notes just the same way the letters C , D , E , F , G , A , and B are used to name the notes in English.

Sound Practice From The Sound Of Music

Sound of music is a beautiful film about music made several years ago. There in the film we see Maria and a group of seven children practice the tonic solfa and making beautiful meanings out of it.

From the film, Maria explains to the children that when we read we begin with A, B and C, but when we sing we begin with Doh, Re and Mi. The first three letters of the English alphabet is A, B and C while the first three notes of music is Doh, Re and Mi.

Then Maria in a bid to help the children understand the tonic solfa, teaches them a song that involves all the syllables of the solfege in an interesting way! Here it is:

Doe (Doh) – A deer, a female deer

Ray (Re) – A drop of golden sun

Me (Mi) – A name I call myself

Far (Fah) – A long long way to run

Sew (So) – A needle put in thread

Lah – A note which follows soh

Tea (ti) – I drink with jam and bread

Interesting isn't it? You can practice the song while you play the different syllables on the keyboard, stating with the first syllable Doh!

Tonic Solfa For Nursery Hymes

CHAPTER SEVEN:

Chords; Major And Minor Chords

Constructing major and minor scales is very important since basic chords in key signatures are built on each degree of a scale. Building chords can also be as powerful piano fingering exercises that help piano players with a developed finger strength and a good knowledge of music theory. As we already know, basic chords, or triads as they are fondly called are constructed on three notes. We use the $1 - 3 - 5$ fingers on both hands to play the chords.

In building chords, there are two possible ways. The first is focusing on building the chords in the context of the keys. Meaning that that we can build chords and move up and down in light of the major and minor keys using the notes found in the scale. The G major key for example, this therefore means that the chords you are likely to play are G – B - D, A –C - E, B –D – F #, C – E - G, D – F # - A, E – G - B and F # - A - C.

The second way we can use to build triads or chords is by using the simple formulas of intervals to build the basic chords found in the major and minor keys. Major and minor keys are constructed on a series of major, minor and diminished chords that do not change.

For example, in C, a major chord could be constructed by just adding E and G, that is, a major 3rd and a perfect 5th.

In minor chords, the mirror expression is the case, the minor chords are actually the mirror of the major chords and not the third of the chord, which is half a step lower. In C minor for instance, the chord is written as C - Eb - G

Below are major and minor chords you can start to practice with;

The Major Chords

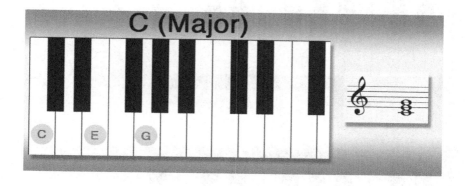

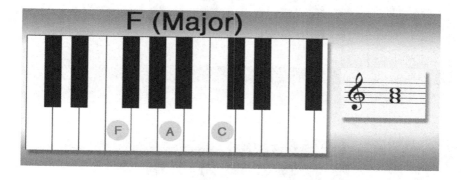

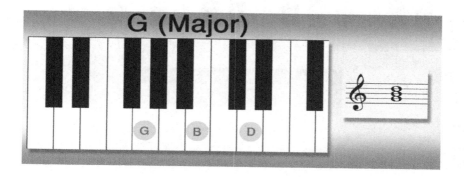

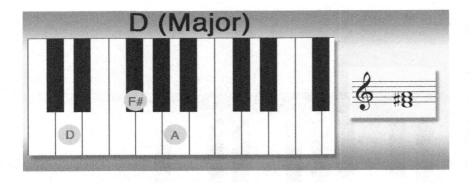

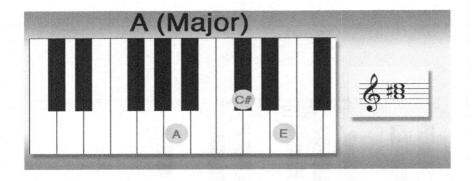

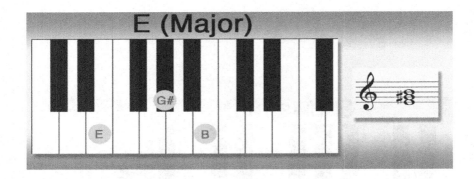

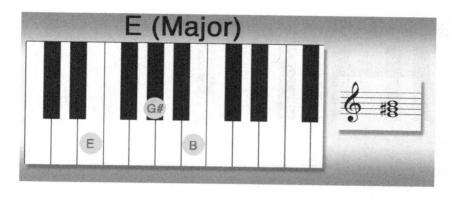

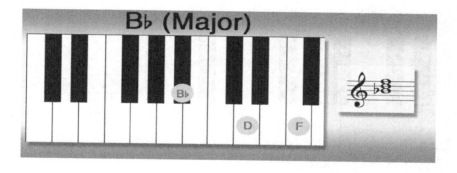

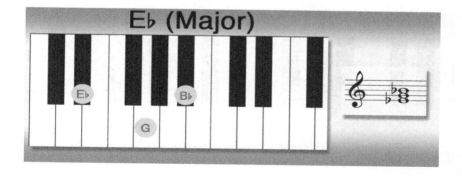

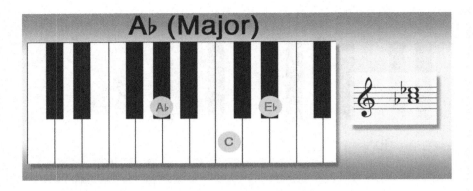

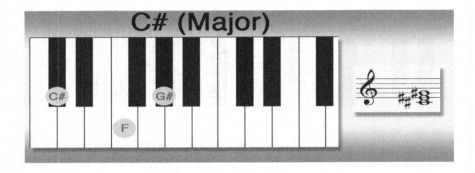

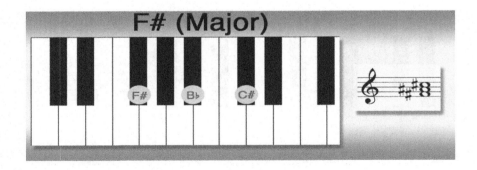

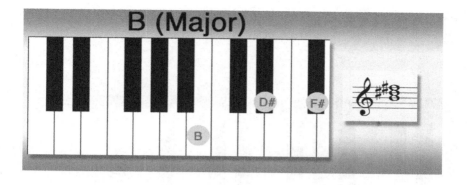

The Minor Chords

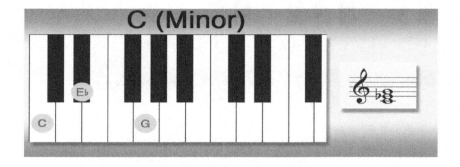

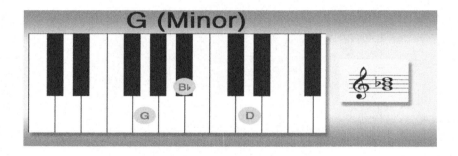

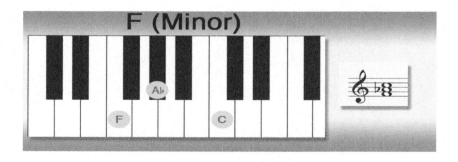

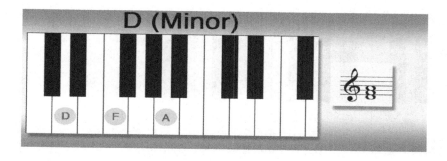

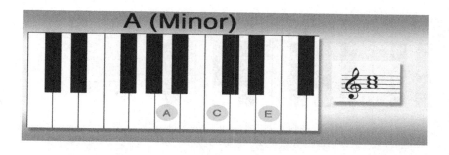

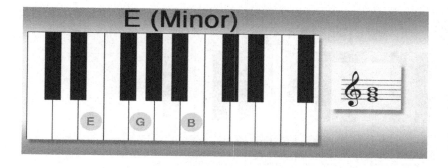

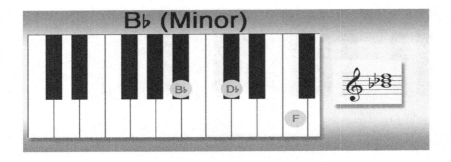

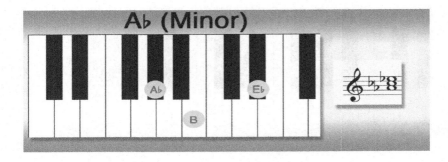

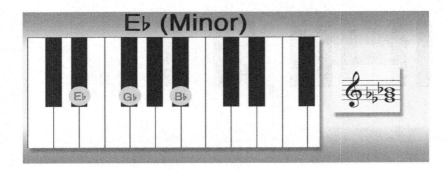

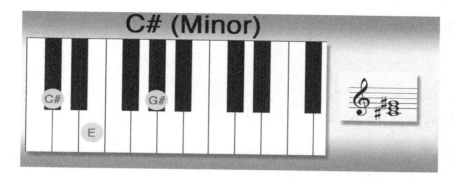

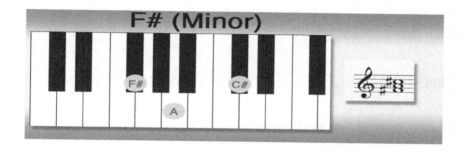

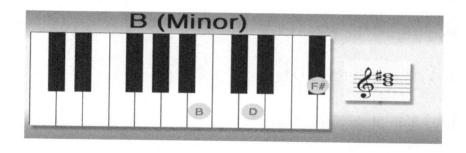

Popular Song

Here are some popular songs and their notes for you to practice with;

ROW ROW YOUR BOAT

Row, row, row your boat

DD D EF #

Gently down the stream

F #EF #A

Merrily merrily merrily merrily

D D DA A AF# F# F#D D D

Life is but a dream

A G F # E D

HAPPY BIRTHDAY TO YOU

Happy birthday to you

A AB A D C #

Happy birthday to you

A A B A E D

Happy birthday my darling

A A A F# D C# B

Happy birthday to you

G G F# D E D

May the good Lord bless you

A A B A D C #

May the good Lord bless you

A A B A E D

May the good Lord bless you —ou

A A A F # D C # B

Happy birthday to you

G G F # D E D